# CONTENTS

*Note*: Wainwright did not draw or even sketch his illustrations whilst on the fells; he took photographs and drew from these later at home. All the landscape photographs in the book are by Wainwright, and the drawings are taken from various books as listed in the Bibliography on pages 205/6.

# Memoirs of a Fellwanderer

© Richard Else

# Memoirs of a Fellwanderer

*a.wainwright*

**F**

FRANCES LINCOLN LIMITED

PUBLISHERS

TO THOSE WHO TREAD
WHERE I HAVE TROD

FRANCES LINCOLN LIMITED
4 Torriano Mews
Torriano Avenue
London NW5 2RZ
www.franceslincoln.com

Originally published by Michael Joseph Ltd 1993

First Frances Lincoln edition 2003

Copyright © The Estate of A. Wainwright 1993

Some of the material appearing in this book is taken from works
originally published by the *Westmorland Gazette*, Kendal.

Printed and bound by Star Standard, Singapore

A CIP catalogue record is available for this book from the British Library.

ISBN 978-0-7112-2239-7

2 4 6 8 9 7 5 3

# FOREWORD TO THE PAPERBACK EDITION

## *by Betty Wainwright*

Now, some twelve years after AW died, I am constantly reminded of how much he gave me. I went recently with a friend to Cartmel Priory. With AW, I had always been the driver, he the navigator (it took me years to teach him to give me warning of a turning to take rather than telling me a split-second after I had passed the road); now I was being driven and was the navigator and the little lanes came back to me as though it were yesterday. Leaving Cartmel afterwards, the first of the mountains in the north came into view. 'What's that one?' asked my friend. Before I could stop to think, I said, 'Coniston Old Man.' And a little later, as we drove up the hill from Newby Bridge, heading for the delightful little fells around Strawberry Bank, she asked again: 'What's that mass of fells over there?' Again I was able to answer without hesitation: 'The Langdale Pikes.' AW had taught me well.

We drove through Crosthwaite at the head of the Lyth Valley, climbed up and over Scout Scar, and started to drop down to Kendal. This is where AW would have said to me: 'Nearly home' – perhaps checking his watch to ensure we would be back in time for *Coronation Street.* Now, with the spring sun lighting up the white of the hawthorn blossom, I said to my friend: 'Nearly home' – and remembered so much.

▶ *Blossom time, Lyth Valley*

# FOREWORD

## by Betty Wainwright

Iwelcomed the opportunity to write the foreword to this book which, combined from AW's two books written over twenty years apart, comes close to revealing the real man; a sensitive, shy man who sought anonymity, hiding himself behind a gruff exterior. It gives a poignant picture of his obsessive love affair with the fells of Lakeland and of his quirky sense of humour. The latter was well illustrated in a letter I received after his death. The writer of the letter was chairman of a committee on which AW also sat. AW had arrived early at the chairman's house for what was expected to be a difficult meeting. In the course of this preliminary discussion, he said, 'Well, Mr Chairman, if I were you I should put them in your dining-room with its lovely vista of the lake. It might widen their horizons.'

Against all odds and totally unaided he followed his star and produced over sixty books starting with the unique Pictorial Guides to the Lakeland Fells. The field work for these seven guides was done at weekends and brief holidays, always using public transport. Often he rode on buses for several hours in order to have just an hour or so of walking. He refused offers of help with transport until he began work on *Pennine Way Companion*. In this part of the world it is easier to travel by bus or train from north to south than west to east, and so, reluctantly, he accepted offers from a few car-owning acquaintances who knew of his plans. I was one of these.

We had first met face to face a few years previously when I was summoned to the Town Hall where he was Borough Treasurer. I was to be reprimanded for signing a form promising payment on behalf of a travelling ballet company who had used the Hall for one of their performances. They were late with their payment and I was told in an avuncular but firm way never to do that sort of

◀ *Blea Tarn*

thing again! I sensed then a gentleness beneath a stern front. The memory of that meeting remained in both our minds.

After one or two sorties to the Pennine Way when I was left to my own devices between the dropping off and the picking up, I had the temerity to ask if I could accompany him. He looked surprised, was silent for a few seconds and then said I could if I didn't talk! And so it began, our comfortable, loving companionship that was to last until the end of his days.

Friendships are forged on the fells; coping with the elements, the hidden hazards and the unexpected happenings reveals the best and the worst in individuals. We grew to know each other well. We both had had unhappy first marriages. I had come to Kendal after an unfortunate first attempt and had been on my own for seventeen years, bringing up two young daughters. AW's wife had left him on his retirement, as she said she would, and he had coped alone for three years. We felt very lucky to be given a second chance.

We were married in 1970 and he promised me ten happy years; I was privileged to have almost twenty-one. Each year was full, active and productive. Even with failing eyesight he carried on without any complaint, and his mental faculties remained as sharp as ever.

Our backgrounds, temperaments and skills were different, but together the combination worked and we made a happy and balanced whole. I was able to stave off unwanted public attention, act as a go-between, protect his peace so he could write and draw undisturbed, look after the house and garden, and transport him and walk with him whenever he wanted to go. He was my rock; totally dependable, utterly honest and often very amusing, with a dry sense of humour. He opened my eyes to an entrancing world, and I was never happier than on our walking days. He encouraged my love of wild flowers, and while he pored over maps at the end of the day, checking our explorations, I identified flora.

Scotland became our other great love. We went again and again for visits that were almost always working holidays, staying in rented cottage accommodation so we could be free to come and go as we pleased. We went everywhere, particularly in the years when he drew all the Munros. One of our favourite areas was Wester Ross, and Plockton became our centre. It is wonderfully situated with Glen Sheil to the south, Skye to the west, the Torridon mountains to the north and the scenic railway from

▲ *Plockton on the south shore of Loch Carron*

Lochalsh to Inverness to the east. Sometimes if the weather had been kind and the work was done, we indulged in a 'pottering' day, beach-combing or revisiting a special place.

Over the years we acquired several cats. All were strays rescued from illness and abandonment. They came to us through our involvement with Animal Rescue, Cumbria, supposedly as temporary members of the household until permanent homes could be found. Somehow they settled in and stayed. Once when a particularly lively kitten was misbehaving I remarked that it was probably time for it to move on. AW looked up from his paper and said, 'He won't like that.' He meant, of course, that he liked the miscreant and wanted him to stay! His especial favourite was Totty, a little scrap of black fluff who was barely three weeks old when she arrived; she had streaming eyes and was unable to lap or walk. With careful nursing she survived to become the boss cat; she sat on his desk during the day and slept on his bed at night. She is now sixteen and she misses him still.

It was during the early years of our marriage that we became members of Animal Rescue, and in due course AW became its chairman. Later, when the books became bestsellers and these and television programmes made AW well known, we found we had more money than we felt we needed. He generously arranged to forego certain royalties which were donated instead to Animal Rescue and the Wainwright Animal Trust. The latter distributed

money to small animal charities throughout the country. The former now has a permanent shelter a few miles from Kendal.

As he said in *Fellwanderer*, AW was not mechanically minded but he loved projects and planning. Holidays and outings were meticulously organised with an A and a B plan. If I asked for a corner of the garden to be re-designed or some new steps to be made there was enthusiasm for the creative part of the job but he was not interested in maintenance. That became my department. I had to change plugs, mend fuses, oil squeaky doors and deal with the car. In my capacity as treasurer of Animal Rescue, I brought home the takings from fund-raising events to be counted and checked. AW helped eagerly with the counting and would put the money into neat piles, but he never got the hang of bagging the coins. Many times, if I hadn't joined him at the outset, I would arrive at the table to find the cats had jumped up and knocked over the piles and we would have to start again!

When in the last three years his sight worsened it meant his fellwalking days were over. We still went out, often taking a picnic to some quiet well-loved spot where he could gently potter, his hand on my shoulder for guidance. He would always ask about the clarity of the view and in his mind's eye could see the range of hills around us. Our last visit to Scotland was in the autumn of 1990 and again he could visualise the scenery wherever we were, even remembering the turns of the roads.

He managed to finish typing his last book on the valleys of Lakeland by touch, knowing the end of the line had been reached by the sound of the bell. Many wrong letters were struck but the work was good enough to be read easily. I had always helped with the proof-reading, doing it silently in the early days. Latterly I read everything aloud to him. This obviously took longer, but it was more accurate and we grew to enjoy it. I also read the gist of the daily papers and any articles or letters I thought would interest him. We each took our own paper, and he always had the *Daily Mail*, mainly to look at Alex Graham's cartoon on Fred Basset. I described that to him until almost the end. Because his mind remained so clear and sharp, he was able to enjoy some television, following it mostly from the dialogue. He was a devoted fan of *Coronation Street*. He renewed his love of radio, listening a great deal to Radio 4 and the football commentaries. He was a passionate supporter of Blackburn Rovers, and would have appreciated their re-emergence in the Premier League.

The last two weeks of his life were spent in our local hospital. I was allowed to be there all the time. His book *Wainwright in the Limestone Dales* was shortly due for publication and Michael Joseph whisked a copy off the presses. I was able to put it in his hands a few days before he died, and as I did so he whispered, 'Read the introduction.' He died on 20 January, three days after his eighty-fourth birthday. It was like the felling of an oak tree.

On 22 March I took him to Haystacks. Peter, his son, would have come but sadly he suffers from rheumatoid arthritis and the climb was beyond his present strength; in his boyhood and early manhood he had often walked with his father. So, for this most important of tasks, I was accompanied and helped by one of AW's oldest friends and former colleague, Percy Duff, and Percy's two sons, Paul and Michael. We left Kendal at 6 am when it was still dark and we were near the summit of Haystacks just before 9 am. No one else was about. The day before had been sullen and wet and so was the day following, but that morning was perfect. The sun rose steadily in a blue sky. I left him as he had requested, beside Innominate Tarn, and the larks sang a song of welcome.

# One

# THE TWILIGHT YEARS

It happens to all of us. Everything comes to an end sooner or later. The time duly arrives when we find ourselves unable, because of physical or mental failings, to do the things we have been used to doing. The cause may be an accident or illness or, more usually, advancing age. In our lifetime thus far we have conducted ourselves to a set pattern of activities, avoided annoyances and irritations, and settled down in a comfortable rut of our own making, living as we wished to live and spending our leisure time in pastimes and hobbies that give us most pleasure.

Then it happens. Some disability occurs to disturb or wreck the even flow of existence, to render impossible a continuation of the routine we have enjoyed without much thought that it could end. But it does end. After eighty years it has happened to me. It's my eyes. I can no longer see clearly or focus properly. I live in a grey mist. There are no sharp images any more. Specialists tell me that the retina at the back of each eye has lost its smooth surface, has fractured and is crumbling. They attribute the defect, rather unkindly, to old age. I find it hard to accept this diagnosis. Old age? People are as old as they feel, and life to me has never advanced beyond springtime. I still have the interests and enthusiasms of a sixteen-year-old: simple enthusiasms, restricted mainly to climbing hills and writing about them. I have no feeling that winter is upon me.

The defect has arisen during the past three years. It first became apparent when I found difficulty in deciphering the small print and symbols of Ordnance Survey maps, always my favourite literature. Then, within months, I was unable to read books and correspondence and, less important, newspapers. I still sit for hours with familiar maps open before me: I know them so well

*◀ A W at home: when the mind's eye has taken over (© Mike Harding)*

that the loss of detail doesn't matter, even as a blur they evoke vivid memories of happy wanderings. Books are of less consequence: I never had much time for reading. Newspapers I bought only for the football results and reports; now the radio serves as well. Letters I receive have to be read to me; I reply to them all, but briefly, writing by instinct in a scrawl of which I would be ashamed if I could see it. From the windows of my home I can still see the hills, but their outlines are indistinct and they have lost their features; here the memory fills the blanks. The mind's eye has taken over.

A worse disadvantage arises when out on the fells, this being a growing inability to negotiate easily the rough mountain tracks I have walked so often and come to know intimately. I can no longer see precisely where I am placing my feet, and it has always been a cardinal rule of mine to watch every step, a rule that has given me absolution from accidents. I have long maintained that accidents in fellwalking invariably happen to people who think they can study the views while moving. If you want to look around, stop.

◀ *The path on*
*Haystacks*

▶ *AW's last visit to Haystacks*
(© Richard Else)

I went up Haystacks recently on a wet day. The rain misted my glasses, but this was not the reason why I slipped and stumbled often. There had been wet days before, many of them, and the path was familiar through long acquaintance. No, the truth I had to accept was that I could not discern the roughnesses of the ground even at a distance of only six feet. I loved the walk. It was great to be on the tops again, amongst the fells, the silent friends I have known for half a century and which never change. But they shed tears for me that day.

It is strange how the years of childhood come back to mind in the twilight years of retirement. During the busy working life one rarely recalls its beginnings, current affairs occupying the thoughts almost exclusively; but now, over a gulf of time, I find myself remembering the circumstances of my upbringing far more clearly than the working years. Much of my middle life has been forgotten: there are gaps in my recollections, but I recall vividly the happenings of infancy and boyhood and youth.

## *Two*

# BOYHOOD IN BLACKBURN

Life did not start too well for me. I was born and brought up in Blackburn in a small four-roomed cottage, two up and two down, in a terrace of like dwellings, with flagged floors, no garden, no bathroom, a privy in the little backyard, the living room wallpapered and the others lime-washed. The one table was covered by oilcloth, tacked down at the corners, a tablecloth appearing only on Sundays. Suspended from the ceiling was a clothes rack that could be lowered by a pulley to the front of the fire on washing days. We had an aspidistra, like everybody else: a poor specimen with more dead, brown leaves than green. The front door opened directly from the pavement into the living room and neighbours entered without knocking, often to my discomfiture when I was in a tub on the hearth. There were cockroaches in residence under the big black oven and firegrate, mice appeared occasionally and were cruelly despatched by a mousetrap; a sticky flycatcher hung from the gaslight and was black with casualties. These conditions were common; there were many thousands of similar tenements in the town and all of my youthful pals came from such homes.

Looking back, I suppose we lived in poverty, but so did everyone else I knew. Meals were often jam butties, varied by chips when funds allowed, but there was always something special on Sundays: a joint of beef and jelly; I loved jelly and it was my privilege to scrape the dish clean. Wages were low and there was unemployment. Everybody accepted the conditions in which they lived,

▼ *The house in Blackburn*

having known nothing better. Neighbours were kind and helped each other. There were no complaints, no protests.

These were the bad old days we so often hear about. But were they bad? There were no muggings, no kidnaps, no hi-jacks, no football hooligans, no militants, no rapes, no permissiveness, no drug addicts, no demonstrations, no rent-a-mobs, no terrorism, no nuclear threats, no break-ins, no vandalism, no State hand-outs, no sense of outrage, no envy of others – or, if there were, we never heard of them. Life in adversity can at least be placid. Bad old days? No, I don't agree. People worked hard; they had pride, courage, character, honesty, and an observance of moral standards not seen today. These virtues have been largely destroyed by the Welfare State, a good concept with evil side effects: it has bred laziness and a new race of scroungers. People don't fend for themselves as they used to have to do; new generations have developed that do not work out their own salvations but depend on the State to provide for them as a right to which they are entitled. 'From the cradle to the grave' is interpreted literally. If State benefits are available they are grabbed without a blush. Why work if there is no need to? In the old days it was a matter of shame to live on charity and only the real unfortunates did so. But no longer. Shame and conscience are forgotten words.

Things were not easy at home. I was the baby of the family, with a brother and two sisters much older than myself. My father, a stonemason, was an alcoholic when he had any money but had long periods of unemployment. On the occasions when he was earning a wage, my mother or one of my sisters would waylay him as he was leaving his place of work on Friday afternoons to try to get some money from him before it was all spent on drink.

▼ *First portrait of AW, and his mother and father*

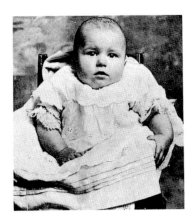

◀ *Sisters Annie and Alice, and brother Frank with a friend*

I had great compassion and love for my mother, who had come from a good family. She had few comforts. To earn a few extra shillings she had to take in washing from rather more affluent neighbours, and I was often awakened during the night by the sound of the mangle downstairs in the kitchen. She always saw that her children had enough to eat, but I noticed at times that she went without herself. Every Friday evening a lady in a fur coat called for the rent of six shillings a week, and I cringed with shame on the occasions when my mother had to say that she could not manage to pay the rent that week but would settle the arrears as soon as she could. I wished I was old enough to go to work to help my mother, or find a buried treasure. But there were no buried treasures in Blackburn in those days and none above ground either.

Almost every adult worked in the cotton mills. I remember, as a child, lying in bed in the early mornings, the stillness of the night broken by the knocker-up on his rounds as he tapped on the bedroom windows along the street with a long stick. His visits were followed by a half-hour's silence and then came the first clatter of clogs on the pavement outside, this noise gathering momentum and growing in volume, rising in a crescendo for five minutes before dying away as suddenly with an occasional hurried scurrying by those late for work. Then the mill hooters sounded, like sirens calling the faithful to prayer, some whining, some whistling, some screaming, some tremulous, some thunderous and frightening in the darkness of a winter's morning. I came to know all the mills by the sound of their hooters, all distinctive; they signalled the start of work at 6.30 (later 8.15).

Life was grim for the employees in the mills. The work was

hard, the noise of the looms deafening; conversations were carried on by sign language and grimaces, but there was great good humour, with much fun at the expense of the overlookers, known as tacklers. At the end of the working day there was the same cacophony of clogs passing the house, but now less hurriedly, more wearily. A few more shillings had been earned.

Sundays were different. The Sabbath day was special. The mill hooters were silent; there was no clatter of clogs. Most people went to church or chapel, or, if they did not, respected those who did. My father, to his credit, never went drinking on Sundays and stayed indoors. People wore their best clothes, the men appearing in suits, often shiny with age; hats were replaced by caps, and a few men even sported bowlers. But it was the womenfolk who transformed the scene. Many were unrecognisable on Sundays; during the week I had seen them shuffling along the pavements draped in long shawls, with thick black wrinkled stockings and clogs, like ghouls going to a funeral. On Sundays they became butterflies, with a lifespan as brief, wearing hats adorned with wax flowers and fruit, smart costumes and dresses; silk stockings covered legs that had seemed shapeless, and neat shoes took the place of heavy clogs. On Sundays women became ladies.

There was much gaiety, people smiled and greeted each other. The Sunday ritual included a walk to the public park a mile away where there were trees and flowers and birds. Everybody paraded the paths around the artificial lake or sat on the seats to watch the processions pass; occasionally there were band concerts. The park, deserted during the week, presented an animated scene, older people renewing acquaintances, while for the young it was a day of courtship. All looked forward to Sundays.

We were a close-knit and insular community, with few interests outside the town's boundaries. Most of the millfolk had a week's holiday in Blackpool each summer after saving up for it for twelve months, and the autumn illuminations on the promenade there later provided an evening's night out at the cost of a half-crown coach journey; otherwise few people had occasion or opportunity to get away from their environment. We knew little of the happenings in the outside world. We did not take a newspaper at home, wireless sets had not been invented, and our main source of information was the newsreel at the cinema. The only event of national concern that I remember from the early years was the sinking of the *Titanic* in 1912.

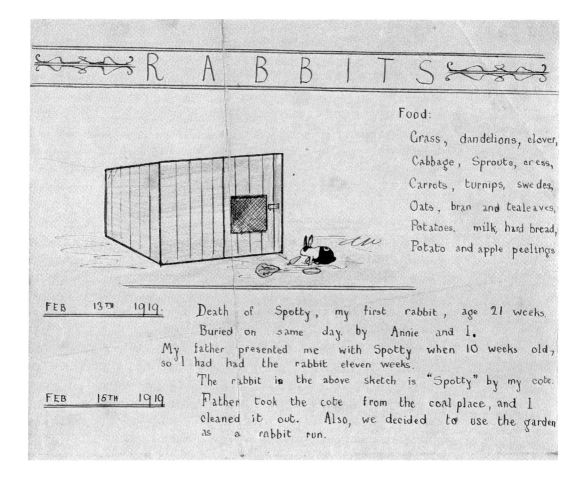

~~~~~R A B B I T S~~~~~

Food:

Grass, dandelions, clover, Cabbage, Sprouts, cress, Carrots, turnips, swedes, Oats, bran and tealeaves, Potatoes, milk, hard bread, Potato and apple peelings

FEB 13TH 1919: Death of Spotty, my first rabbit, age 21 weeks. Buried on same day by Annie and I.
My father presented me with Spotty when 10 weeks old, so I had had the rabbit eleven weeks.
The rabbit in the above sketch is "Spotty" by my cote.

FEB 15TH 1919 Father took the cote from the coal place, and I cleaned it out. Also, we decided to use the garden as a rabbit run.

Unemployment and poverty savaged the decency of people, made the young old too quickly. But I was not unhappy, and not different from my playmates. None of us ever had two pennies to rattle together but we managed to have fun.

I was one of a gang of young ragamuffins who gathered on summer evenings to kick a rag ball about on a cinder track nearby. When the weather was too hot for energetic pursuits we played marbles in the gutters or lay in the street pricking the bubbles of tar among the granite setts, or hunted caterpillars on the elder bushes among the henpens in the back lanes, keeping our captures in matchboxes. Like all small boys we were guilty of acts of cruelty, pulling the wings off bluebottles and the legs off spiders. Sometimes one of the gang would produce a home-made kite and off we would go to a vantage point to see how high we could make it fly.

On winter nights the meeting place was the gas-lamp at the corner of the street, where we invented games on the pavement but were always on the lookout for diversions: if we heard of a building on fire we went to watch; if there were roadworks nearby we stood around the brazier of the nightwatchman outside his little hut. We often trooped along behind the lamplighter on his visits to all the gas-lamps in the street with a long stick that had a flare on the end. The universal practice of small boys in those days was the collection and swapping of cigarette cards, called fag cards, and any man who came along smoking a cigarette was a target for enquiry: 'Got any fag cards, mister?' We had one enemy: at seven o'clock each evening a huge policeman with a ginger moustache came along the street on his beat and his approach was a signal for the gang to disappear. We weren't doing anything wrong but he might have thought we were and we didn't want to be sent to prison. We regarded P.C. Sanderson with great respect.

These varied entertainments cost us nothing. The only money any of us ever had was a penny spending money each week, and this was reserved for the 'penny-rush', the Saturday afternoon matinée at the local cinema, more often referred to as the flea pit, where a howling babel of cheers and shouts and boos accompanied the exploits of Pearl White, Stingaree and W. S. Hart. Every day had its fun and excitement and was never dull or boring. There can be happiness with empty pockets.

On wet nights I stayed indoors, sitting by the window, keeping a census of all who passed in various categories: pedestrians, cyclists, horses and carts; motorised vehicles were too few to be worthy of record. During the winter I would write and illustrate adventure stories on any blank pieces of paper I could find, but my greatest joy was to copy drawings and cartoons from the comics that circulated amongst my pals. Some of these early efforts, done when I was about ten years old, have survived the seventy years.

In some small respects I was different from my youthful friends. I must have been a throwback to a forgotten ancestor, for alone in the family I had a thatch of fiery red hair, an embarrassment that led me always to wear a cap when out of doors to avoid or minimise the shouts of 'Carrots' that followed me along the streets. At school I was a bit brighter than the others in the class. We were all ragged urchins in the patched and cut-down clothes

of older children in our families: I wore the discarded blouses of my sisters and the short trousers of my brother throughout my years at the Board School. We were a motley bunch of young-sters, very like Ken Dodd's juveniles; many had candles hanging from our noses, removed on occasion, in the absence of handker-chiefs, by our sleeves.

The teachers, however, were all smartly dressed and they were kind. I remember them very clearly although other people I met and worked with in later years are forgotten. They seemed to like me more than the others: they lent me books to read at home and sometimes gave me a threepennybit when they were especially pleased with my work, rewards I dutifully and proudly handed to my mother: a threepennybit equalled a loaf of bread. Everybody except the teachers wore clogs with iron caulkers and ran to and

from school striking them on the flagged pavements to make sparks; another source of free entertainment.

I was different too in my liking for solitary walks. It all began when someone gave me a map of Lancashire, a tattered sheet on a small scale but it opened a bit more of the world for me, and I was eager to learn. For the first time I could see the surrounding towns and villages of which I had heard in relation to Blackburn, and the roads linking them. I treasured that old map and studied it intently, planning walks to places new to me. In due course I walked all the roads and visited all the urban communities within reach, but I was especially attracted to the land coloured brown on the map indicating land over 1000 feet. In these areas, there were no roads and few habitations; they were wildernesses in my youthful imagination, places to explore. I ventured on all the nearby hills and moors: Longridge Fell, Pendle Hill, Hambledon Hill, Darwen Tower, and always with the summits as objectives. Some of my performances were remarkable for a little lad. Ill shod and ill clothed, with jam butties in my pocket and no money for tram fares, I often tramped twenty miles in a day's walk, interested in all I saw; I liked looking around corners at fresh scenes.

These early excursions out of sight and sound of the towns bred in me a love of lonely uplands that has persisted ever since, and a fascination for maps that has never faded; I found an absorbing pleasure in making meticulous copies of them, some adorning the classroom walls long after I had left school.

There was a war going on about this time – the First World War – and everybody was scared and fearful. Zeppelins were coming over at night and dropping bombs, and although we sometimes heard the drone of their engines in the darkness Blackburn was never a target and our main concern was the fighting in France.

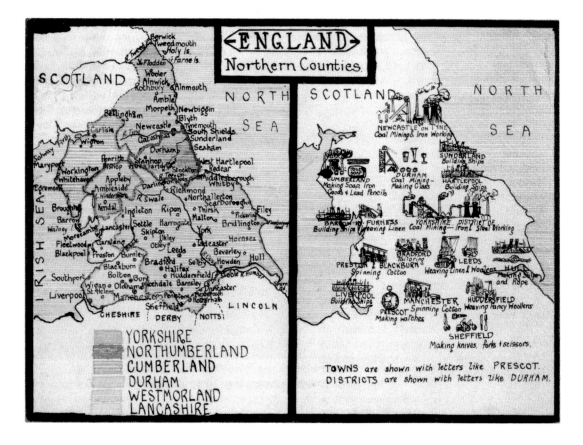

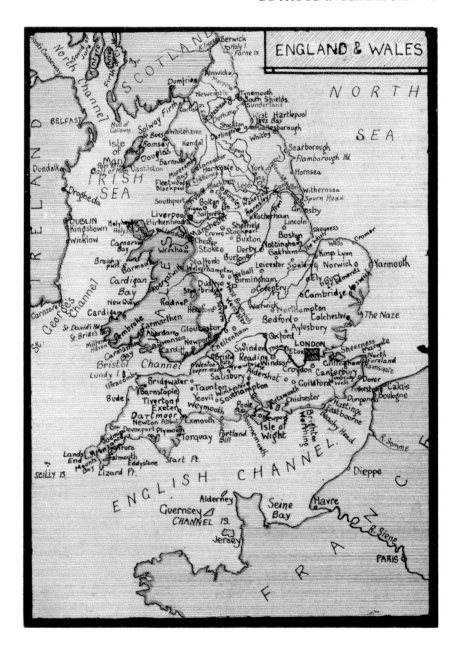

My father was drafted to munitions and was away from home for long periods, his absence being a relief to all of us. My brother, Frank, was called up for service in the Army, and we were immensely proud when he was promoted to lance corporal, but his long silences were a constant worry and my mother prayed every day for his safe return. He was wounded but not seriously and finally came back to the fold. I had worshipped my big brother before he went away, but now he was a man and had changed. He began drinking heavily, to my mother's secret distress, which she never voiced, but I noticed a new sadness in her eyes.

◄ *Frank, home from the war*

It was traditional for youngsters to start work in the cotton mills, half-time at first, upon reaching the age of twelve. I rather fancied myself as an office boy. Sitting at a desk seemed to me preferable to standing at a loom and although I didn't know anybody who worked in an office and had little idea of the nature of the duties, I liked writing and was good at sums, attributes I thought would be necessary and, besides, office work was considered superior, pay was higher and working hours shorter.

My teachers too thought I shouldn't go into the mills but urged me to continue my education at a higher elementary school in the town centre. The prospect appalled me. This was a much posher school, standards were higher and I might be a dunce. I wouldn't know anybody there, the boys came from better homes, and the move would involve expenses of shoes, decent clothes and tram fares on wet days, expenses I knew my mother could not afford without further sacrifices. But although she would have welcomed another wage in the house, she wanted me to go. So I went in great trepidation, feeling I was cutting adrift from my pals and things familiar, and going into the unknown. I need not have worried. I feared I might be inferior to my classmates; instead, in my first and only year at the elementary school I was top boy in the class in every subject except chemistry and physics, which I never really understood.

## COUNTY BOROUGH OF BLACKBURN EDUCATION COMMITTEE.

# HIGHER ELEMENTARY SCHOOL.

**Half-Yearly Report.—Ending** *march* **19** 20

Name of Scholar *Alfred Wainwright*

Number in Form **20**

Position in Form **1 (90·6%)**

| SUBJECTS | Marks Obtained | Maximum Marks | Position in Form | REMARKS | Teacher's Initials |
|---|---|---|---|---|---|
| SCRIPTURE OLD AND NEW. | 47 48 | 50 50 | 1 | Excellent work done always. | Ex. |
| ENGLISH— | | | | | |
| Reading & Recitation | 49 | 50 | 1 | Three excellent results. | |
| Literature | 44 | 50 | 1 | Apart from twenty in one | R |
| Grammar and Composition | 49 | 50 | 1 | answer no criticism is necessary. | |
| History | 47 | 50 | 1 | Very good indeed. | M |
| Geography | 43 | 50 | 2 | Very good indeed. | |
| MATHEMATICS— | | | | | |
| Arithmetic | 50 | 50 | 1 | His work always shows intelligence | |
| Algebra | 49 | 50 | 1 | and is worthy of the highest | Ex |
| Geometry | 48 | 50 | 2 | praise. Results most creditable | |
| SCIENCE— | | | | | |

*Three*

# THE BOY BECOMES A MAN

Just one year later, when I was thirteen, I was told of a vacancy for an office boy in the Borough Engineer's Department in the Town Hall. Against the advice of the headmaster, who wanted me to stay at school until I was sixteen but didn't know the conditions at home, I applied, was interviewed and given the job at the magnificent salary of fifteen shillings a week, almost a man's wage. I ran all the way home to tell my mother, who was pleased and relieved to have more money coming into the house. My spending money increased from a penny to 1s 3d a week, a penny in the shilling being the customary reward for wage earners. This was affluence indeed; I was beginning to feel like a man. I would now be able to go to a better cinema, and attend the Rovers' matches instead of having to stand outside the ground trying to assess the scoring from the shouts of the crowd inside. New doors opened for me. Dreams became realities.

I went to work on the first day trembling with fear. What if I was no good at the duties I was given to do? What if I got sacked? And I would be in the company of grown-ups, a new experience fraught with unwelcome possibilities. But again I need not have worried. The men in the office made fun of my red hair but were kind and helpful. On the first day, the head of the office took me aside and told me to wear a tie, I having appeared in a celluloid school collar fastened by a naked stud; my brother gave me a tie and there were no further rebukes. My duties were simple, mainly running errands, and I was soon accepted as one of the staff and shared the confidences and conversations of the others. They were a grand bunch of fellows. I can recall them so clearly as I write. I enjoyed going to work every day and being amongst adult company. Work was better than school. And I had money to rattle in my pocket.

I have mentioned my embarrassment about the colour of my hair, and there were two others as I moved into early adolescence. I noticed while at the elementary school that my eyes were not very strong: I had to sit on the front row in the class to decipher clearly the writing and figures on the blackboard. At the cinema I had to occupy a front seat to be able to read the captions of the silent movies. In those days there was a silly stigma about the wearing of glasses by young people; it was said that a boy who wore glasses would never get a girl, and vice versa even more so. But I had to do something: I was having difficulty in the office. So, when I was sixteen, I scraped together a guinea and went to an optician, who provided me with a pair of spectacles: I chose rimless so that people would not notice them much. The difference they made was remarkable: now I could see the screen quite clearly from the back seats of the cinema, and at Ewood Park I could distinguish the individual players. Glasses have served me well with an occasional change of lenses, and only recently have they been unable to correct my failing eyes.

The other embarrassment I suffered was the change from short trousers to long which, anticipating the jeers and comments that would follow, I delayed until the passing of time left me no choice. At the age of sixteen I was already six feet tall and as thin as a rake, with spindly legs emerging from trousers that ended at the knees. I was becoming a source of public amusement. So I took the plunge, got a pair of long ones and after skulking along the back streets for a few weeks to avoid ribaldry and laughter, began to like them. They gave me new confidence. Now I really was a man.

After three very happy years in the Borough Engineer's Office I was transferred, against my wishes, to the Borough Treasurer's Department where, I was told, the prospects of advancement were better. My ambition at this time was to earn a salary of five pounds a week, a target more likely to be achieved by the move. I took a sad farewell of my colleagues in the Engineer's Office, all of whom had become friends, and entered the more sober atmosphere of the Treasurer's.

At first I regretted the change. I was the odd man out and felt decidedly inferior. The staff here were from middle-class homes and all had a grammar school education, and there was much talk of professional examinations. I found the senior members rather condescending but they liked my work and introduced me to the mysteries of accountancy. I missed the happier environment of my former office but quickly adapted to my new duties.

The threat of examinations hung over me like a cloud, however, the main topic of conversation being the preparation and study for them. I did nothing. The examinations cost money and I hadn't any, and besides, unlike the others, I could not get exemption from the preliminary examination because I had left school at thirteen, a grammar school education being necessary for exemption. Then one day the boss sent for me and told me that if I did not take the examinations there would be no further promotion for me. I had been expecting, and dreading, such an ultimatum. Resentfully I started to attend night school, resuming my education in subjects such as arithmetic, algebra, history, geography and English language, subjects I thought I had finished with four years earlier. Going back to school was a humiliation. Dammit, I was a man in long trousers.

▲ *The boy becomes a man*

The professional examinations were nightmare experiences. They were held at Manchester, always in January. This meant getting up early: no problem here because I slept only fitfully the night before, trying to anticipate the questions likely to be asked; a walk to the railway station in the darkness and a miserable train journey, grim-faced, still silently testing my knowledge. No candidates ever smiled on these journeys of inquisition; coming home there were post-mortems and obvious relief. I passed the preliminary examination but only by the skin of my teeth. One question only I answered with total confidence: 'Name the highest mountain in England.' For good measure, I gave the examiner the highest in Wales and Scotland too.

It was a relief to get the preliminary out of the way and feel on an equal footing with the others in the office. Yet although I deplored the effort at the time, my enforced studies were to stand me in good stead in later years, especially of English grammar, which led me to be very critical of the way former friends spoke in conversation. I found myself mutely correcting their many errors of speech and mispronunciations and writhing inwardly at some of their expressions: almost every sentence was punctuated with 'you know' and ended with 'like you know'; verbs were massacred, 'you was' and 'I were' were universal. I suppose I was equally guilty on occasion, but my further studies in grammar purged me, and gradually I withdrew from the company of old acquaintances and preferred to be solitary, no doubt earning a reputation as a snob. I have never lost my Lancashire accent and write much better than I speak. I am still somewhat uneasy about syntax and the tenses, but get by, adopting a rule applicable to all problems: if in doubt, don't do it.

The next ordeal was the intermediate examination of the Institute of Municipal Treasurers and Accountants, introducing subjects such as accountancy, auditing, economics and local government law, all beyond the scope of the night school. I had to take a correspondence course, the cheapest of which cost seven guineas; this I paid in monthly instalments of one guinea. I worked hard at the new subjects, studying in a cold bedroom under a flickering gas jet, and trying to concentrate despite the street noises and sounds from downstairs, which too often included the ravings of a drunken father. I prepared a beautiful calendar for every day up to the date of the examination and every night recorded the number of hours spent in study. This was a work of art in coloured inks; I wish I had kept it. For two years I sacrificed all my leisure time except for weekly visits to the cinema and the Rovers, losing touch completely with my former mates who still gathered at the street corner and had now added the pursuit of girls to their repertoire of pastimes.

Then came the examination, another ghastly experience, but to everybody's surprise, including my own, I passed with flying colours, gaining honours, and was later summoned to attend the Institute's annual conference in Brighton to be presented with my award. I went, reluctantly, never having been south of Manchester before, and was glad to get back on the next train. In the four years following, I passed both parts of the final examination, became a qualified accountant with letters after my name, and acquired greater status and respect.

I enjoyed accountancy. I liked working with figures and proving them accurate by finding them all in balance at year end. There was satisfaction in preparing annual accounts that I knew to be absolutely correct in every detail. I had been taught at primary school to write legibly and keep my exercise books tidy, lessons I never forgot, and it was a fetish of mine, almost an obsession, to keep my ledgers neat, columns of figures being in strict alignment and written narratives as clear to read as typeset print. I took a great pride in my account books and conducted by example a personal rebellion against sloppy work, a prime cause of mistakes and wasted time. Copperplate handwriting, a feature of the baddest of the bad old days, has become a lost art, standards have fallen, and writing has degenerated into untidy and often illegible scrawls. Indeed, in the business world particularly, signatures on letters are often grotesque and impossible to decipher. It is an indictment of the writers that their names have additionally to be typed alongside, a practice that never used to be necessary. It seems to be regarded as a symbol of success to be unable to write distinctly; the higher the ladder is climbed the greater is the inability to do what a child of four can do.

People have lost satisfaction in doing a job well. 'Why bother?' and 'To hell with it' are the modern slogans. In the world of arts and crafts, there are no longer summits of achievement; we are on a downhill course. We have to go back centuries in time to find the best architects, the best builders, the best painters, the best composers, the best sculptors; these men were infinitely superior. They had patience, skill and pride in their work. That's the difference between then and now.

The examinations were some years ahead, however: in the meantime, there were changes at home. The war was over and after the Armistice in 1918 threads were picked up again and the daily grind resumed under a cloud of sadness at the tragic toll of young men in the conflict. In the years that followed, both my sisters and my brother married and left the house. I was totally absorbed by my studies in the later part of the 1920s and went into a shell, having no time for my old acquaintances and very little for my family apart from my mother. To please her, I continued to attend the chapel each week but gained no spiritual uplift from these visits; I was bored and sceptical of religious teachings. I remember little of the decade apart from the disruption caused by the coal strike in 1926 and, of course, Blackburn Rovers' cup final success in 1928: I was invited to the house of a friend who had a wireless set for this special occasion, and we all went mad.

These were the only events of note as life settled down on an even keel. I was growing up and passing out of my teens. There

▲ *The Borough Treasurer's staff at Blackburn.*

was no inflation in money matters. Prices were stable. A packet of cigarettes cost 6d for 10 and 11½d for 20, and these prices continued unchanged for twenty years. A new suit cost fifty shillings. Admission to Ewood Park was always one shilling. You could budget your weekly expenditure exactly to a penny.

My addiction to the cinema continued unabated; for me and almost all the population of the town it provided a welcome escape from the reality of a depressing urban environment, a glimpse of the world outside we were never likely to see. When talking pictures were introduced to the screens in 1929, there was tremendous interest and excitement: the talkies added a new dimension to lives starved of beauty and romance; now there was music and there were songs. Blackburn was slow in adopting this innovation, and a few of us from the office travelled weekly on foot or by tram to Accrington and Oswaldtwistle, where the superior Western Electric sound system was installed. We were captivated. We were witnessing a miracle.

# Four

# INTRODUCTION TO A DREAM

An event in 1930 made all that had happened before of relative insignificance and settled my destiny. I was twenty-three and, having saved £5 from my spending money, which had increased with annual increments, decided to take a holiday away from home, the first holiday I had ever had. Acquaintances had told me of the beauties of the Lake District and I had seen photographs of the scenery, which promised good walking. The Lake District was only sixty miles away, but until now was another world, beyond reach, unattainable. I invested in a map, planned an itinerary and recruited the company of a cousin, and off we went in a state of great excitement, each carrying a shilling haversack. We walked down into the town and boarded our bus with an air of nonchalance as though going away on holiday was quite a usual experience. Inwardly we were a little uneasy: suppose we got lost, or had an accident or were killed on the mountains? We felt like explorers going into the unknown.

Beyond Preston we left the huge factories and mill chimneys behind and passed through a green and fertile countryside, heading for Lancaster, my county town but new to me. Beyond Lancaster the landscape was undulating and more varied. At one point of the journey I got my first ever glimpse of the sea in Morecambe Bay, and rising above its far horizon was a hazy background of lofty hills: a thrilling sight. The Lake District!

The bus took us along the long main street of Kendal and entered a colourful fairyland, the hills now bordering the road with occasional vistas of mountains, real mountains and, on topping a rise, a long serpentine sheet of water fringed by glorious woodlands came into sudden view. Windermere!

Alighting from the bus, our first objective, according to my

*▲ View from*
*Orrest Head*

itinerary, was Orrest Head, a recommended viewpoint nearby. Our way led up a lane amongst lovely trees, passing large houses that seemed to me like castles, with gardens fragrant with flowers. I thought how wonderful it must be to live in a house with a garden. The sun was shining, the birds singing. We went on, climbing steadily under a canopy of foliage, the path becoming rougher, and then, quite suddenly, we emerged from the shadows of the trees and were on a bare headland and, as though a curtain had dramatically been torn aside, beheld a truly magnificent view. It was a moment of magic, a revelation so unexpected that I stood transfixed, unable to believe my eyes. I saw mountain ranges, one after another, the nearer starkly etched, those beyond fading into the blue distance. Rich woodlands, emerald pastures and the shimmering waters of the lake below added to a pageant of loveliness, a glorious panorama that held me enthralled. I had seen landscapes of rural beauty pictured in the local art gallery, but here was no painted canvas; this was real. This was truth. God was in his heaven that day and I a humble worshipper.

The mountains compelled my attention most. They were all nameless strangers to me, although I recognised the Langdale

Pikes from photographs I had seen. They looked exciting and friendly. I fancied they were beckoning me to their midst. Cloud shadows chased across them as I watched, and momentarily they appeared gloomy and frightening, but with the return of the sun they were smiling again. Come on and join us, they seemed to say.

There were no big factories and tall chimneys and crowded tenements to disfigure a scene of supreme beauty, and there was a profound stillness and tranquillity. There was no sound other than the singing of larks overhead. No other visitors came.

My more prosaic cousin went to sleep in the warm grass. I forgot his existence. I felt I was some other person; this was not me. I wasn't accustomed or entitled to such a privilege. I was an alien here. I didn't belong. If only I could, sometime! If only I could! Those few hours on Orrest Head cast a spell that changed my life.

Eventually my cousin roused himself and reminded me that we hadn't yet arranged a lodging for the night. After a last lingering look around, and still in a dream, I went down with him to Windermere Town and in a cottage at the end of a side street I had my first experience of a bed and breakfast establishment. It was a homely and comfortable place, providing supper also, after which I reflected on the events of a memorable day and studied the map to plan the morrow's adventure, disturbed somewhat by another visitor who played the piano all evening.

◀ *AW with his cousin Eric Beardsall*

*Fairfield and Seat Sandal from Steel Fell*

The next day was again sunny and we walked up the Troutbeck valley, still entranced by all we saw and in awe of the towering mountains that soon closed in around us. Near the head of the valley we started our first great adventure. I had noticed on the map a path that led upwards to a high ridge and was marked 'High Street, Roman Road'. I remember vividly, as we toiled up the grassy groove of Scot Rake, halting for a moment to look around and seeing far above us the summit of Froswick, clearly outlined against the blue sky and seeming incredibly high and impossible to reach. Froswick was not like Pendle Hill. Here were not smooth grass slopes but a savage uplift of stones and low crags, an intimidating sight that made us debate the wisdom of proceeding further. Froswick was a real mountain, the first we had ever seen at close quarters, and the aspect was frightening. But the path was easy and inviting and we plodded on ever upwards, duly reached the ridge and all at once looked down into the great gulf of Kentmere Head on the other side, its streams like silver threads far below. There was no doubt that we were embarked on the greatest adventure of our young lives. There had never been a day like this before. Mountains rose all around us,

*▲ View down the Troutbeck Valley to Windermere*

*Thornthwaite Crag from the summit of Froswick*

silent and brooding, and we were innocents in their midst, with nobody around to assure us of our safety. There was a soundless silence, a profound stillness; we were alone in a strange new world except for a few grazing sheep who seemed not at all concerned by the awful loneliness of their surroundings . . .

The walking was easier now and we went on, visiting the tall obelisk of stones on Thornthwaite Crag, comforting evidence that others had been here before us, and then crossed to the long whaleback of High Street, finding and following the faint traces of the Roman road. Of course we had no cause for alarm: the Romans had come this way nearly two thousand years ago. This thought eased our troubled minds,

▲ *High Street*

and when the long serrated skyline of the Lakeland heights came into distant view to the west, our fears were succeeded by a confident exhilaration. It was great being up here alone on the top of the world. Spirits soared: we were gods looking down on a heaven that had fallen upon the earth.

We went on along the ridge in the steps of the Romans for many miles, passing over a succession of cairned summits that revealed new and exciting views, and then with the afternoon far spent and hunger gnawing, decided to descend towards a lake my map promised as Ullswater. The long steep descent to valley level was mainly accomplished on our bottoms: our shoes had smooth soles and did not grip the grass. We had not seen a soul since leaving Troutbeck. We returned to civilisation at Howtown, whence a lakeside road took us in gathering dusk to Pooley Bridge.

My cousin, who had travelled more than I and had acquired a measure of sophistication, wanted to stay the night in a hotel. I had never been in a hotel before: they were too posh for the likes of me. But I was persuaded to follow him through a palatial

*Blea Water Crag, High Street*

▲ *Patterdale Village*   ▼ *The head of Ullswater*

*The Patterdale Valley: St Sunday Crag, Grisedale and Helvellyn on the skyline*

▲ *Ullswater from St Sunday Crag*   ▼ *Helvellyn from Fairfield*

doorway and, despite our dishevelled appearance, we were accepted as guests. I need not have worried. The landlord was a Bolton man and was quick to recognise my accent. He was friendly; we ate well and slept well in luxurious comfort. I was beginning to like hotels.

Another place I had read about and wanted to see was Striding Edge on Helvellyn, and next morning we took a bus to Patterdale and followed a pony route rising along the flanks of Birkhouse Moor above the lovely valley of Grisedale. The weather was less promising, and before reaching the gap in the wall we were enveloped in a clammy mist and the rain started. Neither of us had waterproofs nor a change of clothing. Perhaps it would clear later, we thought: we were already under the optimistic delusion that afflicts most fellwalkers. The path was clear underfoot and we entered a grey shroud with visibility down to a few yards only. We went on, heads down against the driving rain until, quite suddenly, a window opened in the mist ahead, disclosing a black tower of rock streaming with water, an evil and threatening monster that stopped us in our tracks. Then the mist closed in again and the apparition vanished. We were scared: there were unseen terrors ahead. Yet the path was still distinct; generations of walkers must have come this way and survived, we said to each other, and if we turned back now we would get as wet as we would by continuing forward.

We ventured further tentatively and soon found ourselves climbing the rocks of the tower to reach a platform of naked rock that vanished into the mist as a narrow ridge with appalling precipices on both sides. There was no doubt about it: we were on Striding Edge. In agonies of apprehension, we edged our way along the spine of the ridge, sometimes deviating to a path just below the crest to bypass difficulties. We passed a memorial to someone who had fallen to his death from the ridge, which did nothing for our peace of mind. After an age of anxiety we reached the abrupt end of the Edge and descended an awkward crack in the rocks to firmer ground below and beyond, feeling and looking like old men. Perhaps mercifully the mist had obscured the perils of the journey, making it a tightrope in the sky and concealing the consequences of a fall. The rain still sluiced down, making rivulets on our bellies. We sheltered for a few minutes at the base of the crack, recovering from an ordeal we had not expected. My cousin, looking like something fished from the sea, kept looking at me and saying nothing but was obviously inwardly blaming me, as author of the day's programme, for his present misery.

Time was passing, the rain not abating, and we could not stay there amongst the dripping rocks any longer. I assured my reluctant companion that we would soon be on the top of Helvellyn and then it would be downhill all the way. We scrambled up the slope from the Edge, often slipping and stumbling, and emerged at another memorial, from which, on much easier ground, we groped our way to the windshelter formed by a cross of walls, but there was no escape from the deluge. Just beyond was the highest point of Helvellyn, over 3000

◀ *Striding Edge*

feet and the greatest elevation either of us had ever attained. There was a tremor of satisfaction in this achievement but we were quite incapable of raising a cheer. A wide path left the summit in the direction we wanted to go and we walked along it at a better pace, now completely soaked with water squirting out of the lace-holes of our sodden shoes. We had gone some way before I realised that our path was not the pony route marked on the map, but it was obviously much trodden and must lead somewhere. It did. It brought us down to the main road at Thirlspot, the later stages being indicated by white stones, but was not marked by the Ordnance Survey; only later did I discover that the pony route had fallen into disuse.

We tramped the six miles into Keswick. The rain never ceased. In Keswick we presented ourselves at a house in Stanger Street with a bed and breakfast sign, looking like two drowned scarecrows, dripping water from every protuberance and making pools on the doorstep. A lady opened the door and invited us inside. It was here that I had my first experience of the kindness and hospitality of the people of the district, an experience that was to be repeated in every cottage and farmhouse where I subsequently stayed. This lady in Stanger Street was wonderfully solicitous and concerned for us: she was a widow who had retained her husband's wardrobe. She made us take off our soaking clothes, gave us warm towels and then supplied us with jackets and trousers and shirts and socks, ill fitting but dry and warm, taking our own rags away to dry. Then she prepared a large supper and we recuperated in front of a blazing fire before retiring to comfortable beds. That woman was sent from heaven.

The next morning was dry and sunny, the rain having spent itself during the night, and my cousin, scarred by his traumatic traverse of Striding Edge and now suspicious of my further programme, insisted on a rest day; in fact, I had to agree when the lady of the house announced that our clothes were still very damp. After a good breakfast, we ventured into the streets attired in the outfits of the late husband, having decided to stay a second night. We were an odd-looking couple. The dead man's vital statistics were very different from mine: his trousers ended halfway up my calves and his jacket was roomy enough to wrap round me twice; my cousin fared little better. From the stares of the people we passed, it was palpable that we were attracting attention.

▲ *Skiddaw from Burntod Gill*   ▼ *Skiddaw and Skiddaw Little Man from Castle Head*

We spent the day in the unfrequented country lanes of the Vale of Keswick, settling down for a siesta on a grassy bank above Millbeck. It was a glorious day, matched by the superlative beauty of the scenery all around. Skiddaw towered behind us in full majesty, incredibly high above steep heathery slopes, a monarch rising over its satellite heights like a hen with a brood of chicks. But it was the view in the southern arc that riveted our attention, where a long array of mountain peaks formed a lofty skyline around and beyond the sweet strath of the Newlands valley. I identified all the summits from the map and vowed to climb them all someday. I was as spellbound as I had been on Orrest Head; here were trees in the foreground and glimpses of lakes. It was a scene of perfection, of flawless beauty, and I saw it through eyes dim with tears: it was an emotional revelation of splendour far beyond my imaginings. I felt honoured to be witness to such a display. And there was colour everywhere, not garish but gentle and soothing pastel shades, and in the distance a translucent blue haze. And again a profound silence over all.

We walked back to Keswick elated, with enthusiasm running high, to find our clothes not only dry but pressed. The lady of the house was an angel, but of course in heaven you expect to find angels.

In the days that followed I lived in an ecstasy of delight. We climbed to the ridges, scrambled amongst the rocks and reached a few summit cairns. We walked entranced along the valleys and beside the lakes. I was bewitched by everything. Here was harmony without a discordant note, and an indefinable aura of romantic charm, a mystical quality of beauty and tranquillity in alliance. The locals we met and in whose cottages we stayed overnight were all friendly and helpful, and their smiling faces reflected an inner peace and contentment as though their serene surroundings had permeated their philosophy of life.

And especially we marvelled at the freedom to roam the hills without restriction or hindrance. We could wander anywhere above the intake walls of the farms without reprimand: there were no policemen, no keep out notices, no warnings to trespassers as there were at home, but absolute freedom of access. It was wonderful to be able to wander and explore at will. The mountains, which later I came to know as fells, had open

*Eagle Crag and the Stonethwaite Valley*

*Derwentwater from Castle Head*

invitations to all. We walked amidst changing and often dramatic landscapes in a state of perpetual excitement.

Our money lasted well, five shillings being the norm for supper, bed and breakfast in cottages. Towards the end of the week my cousin persuaded me into another hotel, the Black Bull at Coniston where, amazingly, supper, bed and breakfast cost only four shillings. I was confirmed in my liking for hotels. It didn't seem to matter that I didn't talk posh.

The day of our return from paradise came all too soon and could not be delayed. A holiday of a thousand delights was over and a bus brought us back home. My feelings ranged between elation and despondency. Blackburn was just as I had left it, yet I viewed the familiar streets and buildings as though I were a stranger. I liked the place, having known no other until a week before, but I saw it differently; my thoughts were elsewhere. I looked at the cathedral and saw Honister Crag, at the canal and saw the Rothay, at the long streets and saw mountain tracks. I was still under a spell.

I resumed the routine of the office but felt I was only half living. The house seemed even dingier: I was depressed every time I turned the corner of the street and saw it. I knew I had to get away. I wanted to live in a house with a garden. I was still studying hard at the time and did not know any girls and very little about them. But marriage seemed to be a solution. A young fellow in the office had a saying he repeated whenever the subject of the opposite sex was mentioned: 'Women are all alike with a blanket over their heads': no need to be selective. I was not a good catch for any young female. I was shy, sensitive, skinny, ungainly, I had red hair and wore glasses: who would have me? Nobody ever regarded me with admiration. So when one at last showed an interest I married her and left home, not easy in my mind and feeling that I was deserting my mother. Neither of us had any money: our honeymoon cost us two shillings, the price of two seats at the cinema on our wedding night. I was given the tenancy of a Council house, a great improvement: it had a bathroom, hot water, and the windows looked out on greenery.

The marriage was to prove a mistake although it produced a son who won a beautiful baby competition. It was a mistake because I was climbing a ladder to a professional career, but my wife, a mill girl, had no wish to leave the bottom rung. We had little in common then and later nothing. If there are any young fellows reading these lines, my advice is to shop around for someone with similar interests and aspirations. Women may all *seem* alike with a blanket over their heads, but they are not.

Six weeks after the wedding my father died suddenly at the age of sixty-two. My mother shed tears but there was no grief amongst the rest of the family. Had I foreseen this happening, I would never have left my mother and would have found a pleasanter house with a garden for both of us to enjoy. She was now alone in a house that had held six, her only income being a pension of ten shillings a week, more than half of which was needed for rent; clearly she could not subsist on this. I had been

the main breadwinner over the past few years and I felt wretched for depriving her of my assistance when I married. My brother and sisters were in no position to help but fortunately I was now relatively affluent, earning more than £4 a week, twice the average adult wage. I was able to augment her pension and provide her with a small radio. I wished I could have done much more but had committed myself to the responsibilities of wedlock.

She lived quite happily for several years, her great joy being her regular attendance at chapel on Sundays. She died at the age of sixty-nine, badly crippled towards the end of her life by arthritis, no doubt caused by her long hours in a cold and damp kitchen. Many men have claimed to have had the best mother in the world. So do I.

# Five

# HEAVEN FROM A DISTANCE

I still day-dreamed about the Lake District, thinking constantly of its manifold attractions and especially of the mountains. I read everything I could about the area. The WC at home was permanently furnished with a map and a second-hand copy of Baddeley's guidebook. I went back to the fells at every opportunity, taking advantage of the occasional cheap train excursions to Windermere on Sundays or staying overnight when the office was on holiday. Ambitions changed. I no longer sought a top-ranking professional career. I wanted to live amongst the fells or within easy reach of them. There were few opportunities for practising local government finance in rural areas. I applied for vacant positions in South Westmorland and Ambleside but without success, having not then completed the examinations.

It was possible on these day excursions to do a long walk between trains, and I introduced myself to the valleys of Kentmere and Longsleddale which, in those days, rarely had visitors. When office holidays permitted overnight stays, I was able to go further afield into new territory. I never kept a diary of these travels; later I came to wish that I had had the foresight to keep a chronological record.

One such expedition I remember above all others. I wanted to make a first visit to Scafell and Wasdale and particularly to see Lord's Rake, about which I had read many alluring references. I stayed the first night at a cottage in the Duddon Valley, having walked over Walna Scar from Coniston. I never slept well in strange beds, being too excited at the prospects of the morrow, and passed the hours of darkness with a cigarette every half hour as I waited impatiently for the dawn. So I was feeling none too

*The head of Longsleddale*

◀ *Eskdale*

bright when I came down for breakfast. I declined the offer of a
packed lunch, knowing I had to cross a valley called Eskdale and
supposing, in my ignorance, that there would be shops and cafés
there. I went over by Grassguards and had my first sight of
Eskdale. I saw a beautiful valley, a green strath of pastures and
meadows between tawny heights but without habitations other
than a few farmhouses; certainly no places of refreshment. This
was a blow, my breakfast having already worked its way through
my system. I had a long way to go and knew Scafell was a tough
giant, but decided to continue.

I went up by Taw House where I was besieged by a pack of
barking dogs, but they meant me no harm and I climbed to the
plateau below Slight Side. By this time I was tired and hungry.
Slight Side was a daunting object, soaring high into the blue sky
above unremitting steep slopes. I knew from my map that it was
an outpost of Scafell and its ascent was necessary to reach the
higher summit beyond. I was near exhaustion and disinclined for
effort, and was soon able to progress upwards only by clutching
tufts of grass and pulling myself a few more inches up the slope. I
spent three hours on that half-mile to the rocky top of Slight Side,
which provided a magnificent panorama I was too far gone to
appreciate. The walking onwards was easier, along a rising ridge

with startling views down crags on the right. Very slowly I advanced along the ridge, feeling like Hermann Buhl on the final ridge of Nanga Parbat, and after another hour dragged myself up to the summit cairn of Scafell, famished with hunger. I had been chewing grass, but scattered around the cairn was the peel of an orange left by an earlier visitor. I cleaned up his litter by devouring it.

Next came the exciting part of the journey, the magnet that had drawn me here. I had to find the top exit of Lord's Rake, a slanting passage across the face of Scafell Crag that would lead me down to the easier ground below. I went on to the rim of the crags, a terrifying spectacle of plunging rocks, manifestly impossible to descend except by falling down them. I knew that Lord's Rake emerged somewhere on the left and walked cautiously in that direction. I passed an opening in the rocky parapet where a narrow gully split the vertical wall of rock but this was palpably not the place I was seeking; it fell away precipitously. I continued along the edge and came to a much wider gully. I tried to assure myself that this must be the top of Lord's Rake but had grave doubts: this gully went straight down but I knew that Lord's Rake went off at a tangent. I was in a panic and began muttering prayers for safe deliverance. The sun was fast sinking and dusk was closing over the valleys. The upper part of the gully looked reasonably negotiable but I could not see what lay below.

In desperation I started down, testing every step. I had an awful feeling that I was about to get killed. The gully was not too steep but choked with boulders and I made downward progress by dropping from one to the next; at one point an involuntary slide resulted in a cut on my arm from wrist to elbow, but it was little more than a scratch: surprisingly it did not bleed and I wasn't aware of it until later when I was licking

▼ *Peter Wainwright at the top of Lord's Rake, Scafell*

*The summit of Fisher Crag looking along Thirlmere to Blencathra*

*The summit of Helm Crag, Grasmere, with Steel Fell beyond*

my wounds. I was gravely handicapped by my shoes, which had smooth soles and were ineffective as brakes. After agonies of apprehension and fear I emerged from the foot of the gully, still alive, into an amphitheatre of stones fallen from it. On a later visit to solve the mystery of Lord's Rake, I found that the gully I had descended was Red Gill and that the route of Lord's Rake actually crossed this apron of stones at right angles, hugging the base of the cliffs. But on this day I did not recognise it. I was lost, and greatly intimidated by the impending crags. Below the stones the ground fell away very sharply in a steep grass slope interrupted by low outcropping rocks, and with caution now cast to the winds and spurred on by an over-riding desire to survive, I ventured down.

The slope was certainly very steep, and narrowed to a grass strip flanked by hostile crags. At one point to negotiate a rock that barred the way I threw my rucksack down ahead of me and watched it bounce in prodigious leaps before coming to rest far below. I followed, mostly on my bottom, and retrieved it and to my great relief noticed that the slope ended in easier ground a short distance ahead and, with spirits reviving, was soon out of danger. My map told me that I was on Brown Tongue, this being confirmed when a good path materialised, and very slowly, and dead tired, I stumbled down to the valley at Wasdale Head, arriving at the hotel as the last light faded from the sky. I was given a meal at the large table that, in those primitive days, served all guests. I had not seen another walker all day.

The route I had followed from the top of Scafell Crag to Brown Tongue was in fact a discovery, giving a direct descent very much shorter than Lord's Rake and presenting no difficulty to a booted traveller but I have never heard it mentioned nor have I ever recommended it. It remains my secret.

I learned many lessons that day. I learned never to under-estimate the fells; the Lakeland heights are small by Alpine standards but they are tough, and the summits are always further than you think. I learned always to carry food, and always to wear boots.

I enjoyed the early years of the 1930s. There were visits to the Lake District to look forward to, my years of study for the examinations were coming to an end, and I was securely settled at the office. I was at an impressionable age, romantically inclined, and

*Crinkle Crags from Oxendale*

*Langdale Pikes from Lingmoor Fell*

*Summit cairn on Pike o'Stickle, looking to Harrison Stickle*

greatly admired the music of Cole Porter, Irving Berlin and
Jerome Kern and others of that time who produced a conveyor
belt of delightful tunes and sentimental lyrics, tunes you could
whistle and hum with feeling, unlike the rubbish screamed by the
pop stars of today.

In idle moments at the office I provided the staff with a
succession of caricatures of themselves and an occasional hand-
penned brochure under the title of 'This Office of Ours'. Some of
these were very good, heralding the dawn of a literary talent, and
although most ended in the wastepaper basket, a few have
survived.

Towards the end of the decade a new war was threatening and
finally erupted in 1939. These were depressing times. Talk was all
of air raid precautions, fire drill, blackouts, barrage balloons,
rationing. Everyone was frightened. Day after day brought bad
news and there was no escape from it. To create a diversion for
our thoughts, I founded with a friend the Blackburn Rovers
Supporters' Club and acted as Secretary and Treasurer, arranging

Blackburn Rovers Supporters' Club

# MOTOR COACH EXCURSION
# TO WEMBLEY

## West Ham United v. Blackburn Rovers

### Saturday, June 8th, 1940

Coach leaves ADELPHI HOTEL at 8-30 a.m.
Return 10 a.m. Sunday from King's Cross Coaching Station

**Reserved Seat: 31/6**
(Including Lunch—Outward and Return)            No. 1 0

meetings and regular whist drives to raise funds, the highlight of
this activity being a journey to London to watch a wartime cup
final, which the Rovers lost 1–0, adding further gloom. The Club
did, however, introduce me to a friendship that has continued
without faltering to the present day.

Young men from the office were called up and replaced by
women clerks. I was by this time one of the top men in the office,
deemed to hold a key position and thus excused military service. I
joined the Local Defence Volunteers, later the Home Guard, but
my few duties were of a clerical nature and I was not required to
parade in public in uniform, much to my relief. Events worsened.
After the tragedy of Dunkirk all except Mr Churchill expected
and feared a German invasion. We waited, sick with apprehension. There was no escape. Travelling was severely restricted.
Posters asked: 'Is your journey really necessary?' The Lake
District was again a world away and out of reach.

# Six

# THE DREAM COMES TRUE

In 1941, however, and out of the blue, came the chance I had been seeking. A vacancy for an accountancy assistant in the Borough Treasurer's Office in Kendal was advertised at a salary of £275 rising to £315. In Blackburn I was then receiving £350, but I applied, was interviewed with three other candidates, none of whom had my qualifications or experience, and my appointment was a foregone conclusion. The Council started me at the maximum of the grade, £315, in view of the drop in salary, and gave me the tenancy of a Council house with Kendal Castle framed in the front window.

The work at Blackburn had called for much unpaid overtime to keep abreast of the calendar, especially in the wartime years with a depleted and incompetent staff. At Kendal it was dead easy,

◀ *Kendal Castle*

a doddle: I could have done it standing on my head. It was a complete change. For years afterwards I never lost the feeling that I was really on holiday. I walked to the office through green fields and amongst trees beside a river, and there were hills in the distance. Life was good.

A new life started. Kendal folk had a reputation for insularity, and strangers coming to live in the town were called 'offcomers', and they remained offcomers for twenty years before being accepted into the social activities of the community. I experienced this at first: people were friendly but aloof. I also soon noticed that the townsfolk were individual characters, some even eccentrics, with many interests in the arts; back in Blackburn people had been very much to a pattern, suffering the same pressures.

My period as an offcomer was brief, however. Within a few months of arriving in the town, I was asked by the Council to arrange a 'Holidays at Home' programme in accordance with a Government injunction to attract people away from the idea of travelling to distant resorts for their summer vacations. This new duty meant forming committees to help to make arrangements for concerts, dances, cricket matches, competitions and sports, and I recruited the services of local worthies known to be interested in these forms of entertainment and very soon I was on friendly terms with all concerned. I was given a free hand and it was good fun. I was kept pleasantly busy all that summer and each succeeding summer until 1945.

▶ *Kendal Town Hall*

*Summit cairn on Sergeant Man, looking to Helvellyn and Fairfield*

# KENDAL HOLIDAY WEEK AUGUST 3rd to 8th, 1942

## PROGRAMME *of* EVENTS 3d.

The participants in the events were mainly local but I was able to arrange a few scoops through agents, bringing to the town the Don Cossack Riders, the Arcadian Follies, and cricketers of international renown including the Yorkshire openers and dear old Wilfred Rhodes as umpire, together with a few West Indians, the first black men many Kendalians had ever seen. These Holidays at Home were a great success. I prepared the programme brochures and decorated them with Kendal scenes. All doors were open to me after the first summers. I was an offcomer no longer.

The Borough Treasurer died in 1947 after a long illness and I was appointed to the position. There were no problems. If office work can ever be described as idyllic, mine was. I was much more devoted to the office than my home. I went to work eagerly each day, usually being the first to arrive and the last to leave. I was blessed with a good staff of willing workers who never caused any difficulties. I kept my ledgers beautifully, even artistically, accounting for every penny of the ratepayers' money. I was now closely associated with the members of the Town Council and got on well with all of them: there were no confrontations, no unpleasant or disturbing incidents. The Council was composed of

◄ *The Borough Treasurer's staff at Kendal; A W in the front row centre with Percy Duff on his left*

local business men dedicated to the welfare of the town; there was no airing of party political beliefs. Their meetings were held in the evenings, and I found these irksome when my leisure time later became more precious to me, but I attended them all. I had time to spare from other duties and over the years accepted appointments with many of the social and charitable associations in the town. At the time of my retirement I had accumulated the secretaryship or treasurership or both of thirteen voluntary organisations in the town.

The Lakeland fells became, more than ever now I lived on their doorstep, the background to my life, especially that part of them above the intake walls. The rough fell country above the limits of cultivation became, through long acquaintance, my special delight, my pet obsession. I walked in a happy but observant trance all over it. There are many people – shepherds, farmers, huntsmen and followers, rain-gauge readers and surveyors – who know their own particular areas much more intimately, but I doubt there are many who have roamed the whole district so extensively and with the sole object of seeing what there is to be

▲ *High Stile from Buttermere*   ▼ *Langstrath from Eagle Crag*

▲ *Wastwater*   ▼ *Peter Wainwright looking across Wastwater to the Scafells*

*▲ St John's in the Vale*

seen – not the obvious things only but those also that are hidden and those that are nearly forgotten. I followed all the usual paths many times, until I became familiar with every boulder (especially those that could be comfortably sat upon), every streamlet, every bog and every rash of stones along the way, but I preferred most the secret places that had to be searched for, the drove roads and neglected packhorse trails, the ruins of abandoned industries, the adits and levels and shafts of the old mines and quarries, the wild gullies and ravines that rarely saw a two-legged visitor. The beauty of the Lake District is there for all to see. The glory of the mountains is there for all to see who climb. The secrets are for those who wander from the trodden ways.

My weekend wanderings in these silent and lonely places, far removed from the other world that pulsated in five-day spasms starting every Monday, gradually developed within me a close knowledge of the geography of this delectable corner of the country and an increasing attunement to the unique and indefinable atmosphere of Lakeland that adds so subtle a charm to so obvious a beauty. I found this life enjoyable, up here on the quiet summits, not down there in the crowded streets. Up here, I was

able to stand back from a too-familiar environment like a painter before his canvas and view events in true perspective. Friday's worries were seen to be nothing after all. The only things that mattered were immediate: the next foothold, the drifting mist, the darkening sky. Life was challenging and, stripped of its pretences, life was good. With climbing came an uplift, not only of the body but of the spirit and the mind. There was no competition here with one's fellows, no silly jealousies of the man in the next salary grade; one's aspirations were simple and decent. There was no worshipping of false idols on the mountains but, instead, deep awareness of a Creator.

*▲ Peter by the summit cairn on Lingmell*

Even then, only the weekends could be spent on the hills, and they were not enough. The Ordnance Survey map and Baddeley I knew by heart: something else was needed. I started to draw pictures. Not of people, or buildings, or street scenes, not of aeroplanes and trains and things. Of mountains. It was fun at first, then a fascinating pastime, building a mountain on a blank sheet of paper.

Let's do Great Gable as seen from Lingmell, say, in ink, with a pen: what memories it invokes! Gradually is fashioned the domed

▲ *Great End from Styhead Tarn*   ▼ *The Coniston Fells*

▲ *Great Gable and Green Gable above Styhead Tarn*   ▼ *Crinkle Crags*

▲ *Scafell Crag from Lingmell*   ▼ *Wetherlam from Great Carrs*

◀ *Great Gable from Lingmell*

summit, where you have so often relaxed and watched clouds sailing overhead after the labour of the climb; Westmorland Crags, where you once met an old professor who told you how the mountains were formed; the rocky tower of White Napes, this reminding you that you have never yet actually visited the cairn there; the Napes Ridges, a shadowed scar on the breast of the mountain; the South Traverse, where you met that girl you would have liked to see again, but never did; the Sty Head track coming up from Wasdale Head that you have trodden scores of times; the Breast Route where you once experienced a snowstorm in May. Memories crowd in on you as you delicately bring to life on paper the various features of the mountain you have seen so often. Your pen moves through a mist of dreams . . .

Yes, drawing was a good idea. It brought the mountains to my own fireside. I could wander over them seated in an easy chair, on a black winter's night, too. Mind you, the way I did it was cheating. Not for me the patient wait on a fellside boulder for the right conditions, the day-long vigil on the same tuft of grass while the details were faithfully transferred from sight to paper; not for me the carrying up of easel and equipment. Life was too short, too rushed and, besides, it took enough effort to get myself up on the hills without further burdening myself with impedimenta. To see me climbing the last hundred feet on Bowfell, you'd think I was at 25,000 feet on Everest. No, a momentary halt and a clear photograph were enough for me. I was a cheapjack at the game. But I am sure fidelity to the scene has not suffered. A photograph captures the picture as it is seen in an instant of time, whereas a drawing done on the spot takes hours, during which the shadows change shape and position as the sun crosses the sky; and the result, because the human eye cannot register all the detail or comprehend the relationship of a single detail to the whole, even

▼ *Kirkstile, Loweswater*

▲ *Wastwater*   ▼ *The path to Scafell Pike from Esk Hause*

► *High Man,*
*Pillar Rock*

in a thousand quick glances, is likely to be not less accurate. It is
necessary only to remember that the ordinary camera lens tends to
depress verticals and extend distances, and correct these imperfec-
tions. But the detail, and the relationship of one feature to all the
rest, is foolproof. I wasn't aiming to be an artist, anyway. My aim
was to draw mountains, not in a romantic and imaginative sense,
but as they are. Yes, I was a fraud. With me it was the result that
mattered, not the means.

An important happening as far as I was concerned, but which
passed almost without comment at the time, was the publication
by the Ordnance Survey, for general use, of maps of the Lake
District on a scale of 2½ inches to the mile. These were grand.
They fascinated me. The one-inch maps we had had to be content
with before suffered from an absence of detail: they were magnificent maps, magnificently drawn and magnificently accurate, but
on the rough country of Lakeland, where summits and crags and
tarns and streams were bewilderingly crowded in small compass
and where the ground was so steeply sculptured that the contours
almost touched, there was simply not room on the one-inch maps
to show every feature that a walker would encounter on his

travels. And the missing details are important. If a man is trying to get on the top of Scafell from Mickledore, it is no help to carry a map that shows the location of Helvellyn in relation to Ullswater: what he needs is a map that shows him in detail how to get on the top of Scafell from Mickledore, and this the one-inch map could not do and it was no fault of the cartographer: there was no room. But the 2½-inch scale was release from a strait-jacket. It gave more breathing space: it permitted the inclusion of more detail, and particularly important detail in the form of walls and fences which are often the only identifiable and reliable landmarks on the fells in bad weather. Mist in the valleys doesn't matter; on the hills it does and there

is nothing more reassuring than to come across a stone wall and have a map that will pinpoint your position and show precisely where the wall will lead if followed. There is no guide more reliable than a stone wall.

▲ *Steeple from Scoat Fell*

The 2½-inch maps quickened my interest in the detail of the fells, and it was a thirst for this knowledge that led me in due course to use the Ordnance maps on a scale of 6 inches to the mile, which provided still greater detail, such as sheepfolds, boundary posts and mine levels. And, because the 6-inch maps had not been completely revised for a great many years, and were thus in this respect out of date, they presented a fascinating picture of Lakeland as it was around the turn of the century, indicating the roads and paths engineered to serve the mines, quarries and sheepfolds since abandoned. It became a joy to me to trace these old ways by which now-forgotten men had journeyed to and from now-forgotten places of employment. The 6-inch maps quickened my interest, and stimulated my imagination, in industrial Lakeland.

It is hard to believe, as we nowadays walk many of the more desolate daleheads and fellsides, where sheep graze undisturbed,

*The Links of Bowfell, with the Three Tarns at their foot*

*The Scafell range from Whiteless Pike*

that they were once a scene of human activity. Only the ruins of industrial enterprise remain today. Silence is always more profound in places where once there was noise. More people than ever are *walking* the hills, but there was a time, not long ago, when those same hills carried a greater permanent population: not men out for pleasure but men slaving for a living in conditions that now seem appalling. They were the tough men, not the present visitors who today 'do' ten summits a day. Those men had no eye for the summits. Nor time. Nor inclination. There was work to be done, hard work. Nobody demanded of them a four per cent increase in productivity each year. They were on maximum effort from the start. They had to be.

But to return to the subject of maps. An inspiring feature of the larger-scale maps is that they give the illusion that one is covering more ground more quickly. Using the one-inch map, a walker may spend all day frigging about in an area represented by two square inches, especially in a complicated region, and the remaining thousand square inches of the map are merely an encumbrance; with the 2½-inch map he can move from top to bottom or from side to side of the sheet in the course of a day's trek; with the 6-inch map he may need several sheets to keep pace with his marching feet on a long straightforward walk such as the High Street range. There's a satisfaction, hard to define because it is really more of a nuisance, in walking off the edge of one map and on to another.

Have you ever tried to draw a map? For all but the expert map-makers, this means, of course, copying an existing map. There is nothing like it for sheer fascination and concentration. An insignificant mistake can, and will, throw everything else wrong, like putting a piece in the wrong place in a jigsaw puzzle. I love drawing maps. Of Lakeland especially, because I love Lakeland. I like to follow streams up from the valley to their source in the marshes of the upland combes beneath the summit crags, and if I cannot do it on the ground I like to do it on maps, my own maps. I like to stand on a summit and see the valley below as on a map. Maps have always been my favourite literature. I would always rather study a map than read a book, even a map of a place I have never been to and never will. Sometimes I think I should have taken up cartography as a career. But then sometimes I think I should have been a landscape gardener, sometimes a forester. Instead of which, I turned out to be an accountant, sitting in an office all day, working with figures that passed in and out of the mind. The figures that stay there permanently are Bowfell 2960, Pillar 2927, Scafell Pike 3210, and so on.

The Ordnance Survey maps are the official maps and the best of all, but they have always had the defect of being not quite reliable in the matter of footpaths on the fells. This matters little to an experienced walker who prefers, after his first few seasons, to find his own way across high country (thereby savouring the real joy of fellwalking) and depends less on his map. But to a newcomer, the beaten tracks are of vital concern: in bad weather they are often the only tenuous links with the safety of the valleys, the life-lines, and confidence is lost when a path is lost. In the days of the old maps, the defect was a defect of omission: many well-blazed paths found no place on the map. I recall that first dreadful ascent I made of Helvellyn: on the way down I had used the White Stones track, even in those days a popular way up and off Helvellyn, but the Ordnance Survey did not recognise it until their post-war revisions. Their own route, more accommodating for the ponies it was originally designed for, was not a mistake of cartography but had been discarded around the turn of the century and in parts had become indiscernible on the ground. At the time, I was puzzled and continued to be until a second visit in the following year [AW's Whitsuntide Tour of 1931] in better conditions, cleared up the mystery.

There were other examples of good tracks in common use escaping the attention of the Ordnance Survey, and in later years I was stopped times without number on the fells by walkers scratching their heads over their maps and wondering where on earth they were: the path beneath their feet was obviously much-trodden, but where was it on the map? The answer was, it wasn't. Footpaths on the fells are of first importance: they show the way and avoid dangers. Panic turns to confidence when a friendly line of cairns is sighted, when the stones underfoot are scratched white by the tread of many boots, and, on occasion, one is even thankful to see a trail of litter indicating the regular passage of visitors. So footpaths became a personal study, too. If the Ordnance Survey couldn't get them right, I thought I could. I noted all I could find.

The words 'paths' and 'tracks' are almost always used without discrimination, even, as I do, to avoid repetition of the same

*Borrowdale from Thornythwaite Fell*

▲ *Boot, the 'capital' of Eskdale*    ▼ *The old smithy, Kirkstile*

word. But there is a difference, and it should at least be known. Paths are made, tracks are trodden. Paths are planned, tracks just happen. The best examples of paths are the former pony routes and drove roads and miners' and quarrymen's ways: you can often see the rough culverts, the retaining walls that keep the footing in place across a steep slope, the skilful use of contours. Paths are surveyed and engineered with tools. Tracks are made by boots and favour the short cut, the direct course. Paths are seldom made nowadays. The newer walkers' ways are tracks. And the best tracks, which would be more properly described as paths, are those made by sheep. The tracing of sheep-tracks on a fellside is a separate study. I have long thought I would like to plot on a large-scale map the sheep-tracks on a fell, any fell taken at random. But take the Kentmere slope of Harter Fell as an example. This is scarred from top to bottom by the gravelly ravine of Drygrove Gill. If you go up the fell by following the gill, you will count scores of distinct tracks crossing from one side to the other, from one grazing ground to another, with only a few feet in altitude between one and the next. They are perfect tracks, but a shade too narrow for the comfort of humans. They are, in any case, rarely of much use to walkers, whose usual progression is up or down, not across. A sheep-track may traverse the whole width of a mountain without gaining or losing more than a few feet in height. Sheep do not like going up or down, and since their function is not to climb mountains but to eat grass they show good sense by performing it with as little effort as possible. It is often amusing to see how boulders and other obstacles to horizontal progress are circumvented, and how persistently the same contour is maintained in the crossing of a deeply-cut beck. Their tracks are centuries old: small dainty feet have pattered along them since long before human walkers came upon the scene. Today we see the principles of the sheep-tracks adopted in the construction of motorways. Our skilled engineers are learning the lessons the stupid sheep have always known. The sheep-tracks are the oldest highways on the hills, and the best. Sheep are neat, delicate, gentle, in all things. If you didn't know that, their footways on the mountains would tell you so.

Salaries had increased as a result of wartime inflation and the promotion to Borough Treasurer of Kendal raised mine from £600 to £900, sheer affluence. I had a house built with the help of a

*The path on Crinkle Crags*

100% mortgage. It was on the edge of Kendal Fell, looking over the valley of the River Kent to the Lakeland mountains and with a far-reaching panorama across Shap Fells to the Howgills. The site was a patch of grass used as a hen run and was bare of other vegetation. I prepared a five-year plan for the garden in glorious technicolor. I planted native trees, far too many as events proved, laid sinuous paths after the style of mountain tracks, made little hills and built cairns on them and created low crags with piled up boulders. I tried to make the garden into a miniature Lake District.

By working feverishly every free evening, summer and winter, I completed my five-year programme in two years and was suddenly at a loss for something to do. I had read all the mountaineering classics in the Public Library many times, especially those of the early expeditions to Everest. I read them all again, then switched to westerns for six months. But I felt I was wasting my time. For years the idea had been nagging at me that I really ought to be paying my debt to the Lakeland fells which had continued to give me so much pleasure and which I now knew intimately. The only way I could express my gratitude was by writing about them. I prepared a plan for a series of illustrated guidebooks, a labour of love that would occupy all my leisure hours until I was due to retire from the office. It was then 1952 and I was forty-five. The possibility that an illness or accident might interrupt or defeat this aim never once occurred to me; I was getting on in years but regular expeditions on the fells had kept me fit. I had never been a fast walker, preferring to stop often and look around, and had become rather ponderous. I weighed 9½ stone when I came to Kendal, at a time of rationing, but a very contented life had since swollen me to 15 stone. No time to lose. I made a start and was immediately obsessed, continuing so for thirteen years until the last page was penned. During this time my hair changed colour from red to grey and then white.

# Seven

# A LOVE-LETTER TO THE FELLS

It was total love of the fells, a desire to escape from the common round, my long-standing fascination with maps, an acquired interest in drawing, an insatiable urge to look round the next corner on a trodden way if I could find one and it didn't matter if I couldn't – it was these things that caused me on the evening of 9 November 1952 to pen my first page in what I intended to be a series of seven guidebooks to the Lakeland fells, each covering a defined area, and, if you are interested, the first page I did depicted the ascent of Dove Crag from Ambleside. I forgot to mention earlier that I have patience. I knew the work would take all my spare time for the next thirteen years, but it was a prospect I smacked my lips over. Somebody once said (it would be a Chinaman, of course) that a journey of a thousand miles starts with the first step; 9 November 1952 saw my first step. It was a good evening for me. It was a winter's night, but I spent it going up Dove Crag and was lost to all else. And the nights that followed were equally good. At that time I had no thought of publication. I was working for my own pleasure and enjoying it hugely. I was gathering together all my notes and drawings and a host of recollections, and putting them in a book so that when I became an old man I could look through them at leisure, recall all my memories, and go on fellwalking in spirit long after my legs had given up.

One thing worried me, however, this being the writing of the notes accompanying the illustrations. I had adopted a bastard style of hand-printing in an attempt to produce the same legibility as metal type set by machine, but I didn't take the trouble, and it really is trouble, to get alignment at the right-hand side. It was easy enough to start at the left-hand side, where it was necessary

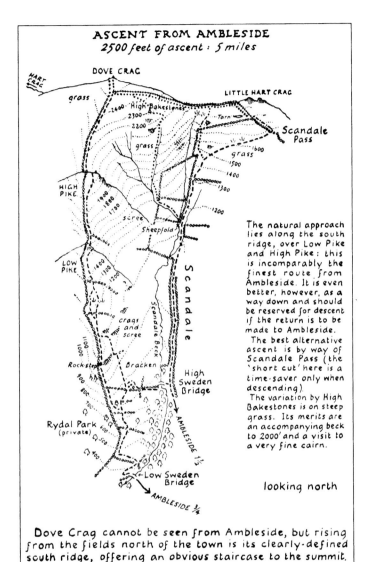

ASCENT FROM AMBLESIDE
2500 feet of ascent : 5 miles

DOVE CRAG

HART CRAG

grass

2400 ··High·Bakestones
2300
2200
grass

LITTLE HART CRAG

Tarn

Scandale
Pass

HIGH
PIKE

1900
1800
1700

scree

Sheepfold

grass
1600
1500
1400
1300

1200

LOW
PIKE

1400
1300
1200

craqs
and
scree

1100
1000

Rock step

Bracken

High
Sweden
Bridge

800

700

Rydal Park
(private)

600

500

400

300

Low Sweden
Bridge

AMBLESIDE ¾

AMBLESIDE 1½

Scandale Beck

Scandale

The natural approach
lies along the south
ridge, over Low Pike
and High Pike: this
is incomparably the
finest route from
Ambleside. It is even
better, however, as a
way down and should
be reserved for descent
if the return is to be
made to Ambleside.
   The best alternative
ascent is by way of
Scandale Pass (the
'short cut' here is a
time·saver only when
descending).
   The variation by High
Bakestones is on steep
grass. Its merits are
an accompanying beck
to 2000' and a visit to
a very fine cairn.

looking north

Dove Crag cannot be seen from Ambleside, but rising
from the fields north of the town is its clearly-defined
south ridge, offering an obvious staircase to the summit.

only to start under the start of the line above, but it was deuced hard to finish a line exactly under the finish of the last word of the line above, and I didn't make the task any easier by deciding I would never break a word with a hyphen at the end of a line. Did these things matter? Not really, I suppose, but the pages looked untidy with the end of the lines staggered, and this began to annoy me. So much so that in July of the following year I scrapped the hundred pages I had then done and started to do them again more meticulously, practising my wording until the lines fitted, or as nearly as I could make them. I never quite succeeded, but the pages looked better then, neater and tidier. They must have done because some readers have not yet realised that the finished books are not printed in the usual way.

The contrary is true. Not a single letter of printer's type has ever appeared in any of them. Subsequently, when it was decided to publish, I was a bit insistent about this. I didn't want a printer interfering with my lay-outs and arrangements. I wanted every page to be exactly as I penned it. I did everything by hand so that each page could be photographed and reproduced exactly. Another consideration was cost. It was cheaper to do it this way.

   This brings me to the financial aspect of the venture, about which many aspiring guidebook writers have addressed anxious questions to me, and since the story has already appeared in print,

*◀ Newlands Church*

through what I regard as a breach of confidence, I may as well repeat it.

By the time Book One was finished, I had begun to feel that other walkers also suffering from, or rejoicing in, Lakeland fell fever, might find some use for it. Perhaps I could be an accountant and an author too. I had become quite fond of my little infant, but it was a poor frail thing and I daren't risk exposing it to the mercies of a publisher. I couldn't face the probability of rejection. That would have hurt, and anyway publishers aren't fellwalkers and wouldn't understand. What did they know of Sharp Edge who sat at a London desk? What did they know of mountain silence who lived in a world of tumult? So I took it to Sandy Hewitson, a local printer. Sandy wasn't a fellwalker either, in fact with only one leg he couldn't be, but he was a better man than most with two: and he was a craftsman who saw in the job a challenge to his ability. I asked him how much it would cost to make copies. He said, how many copies? I thought I could reasonably expect to sell 500 – you can always find 500 people ready to try anything once. Costs were worked out – 500 was clearly uneconomical. It had to be 2000 to bring the unit cost down sufficiently to permit a reasonable selling price. I asked how

*Loft Crag, Great Langdale*

*Summit of Coniston Old Man, looking to the Scafell range*

▲ *Kentmere Church*

much 2000 would cost. Sandy said £950. I said I had only £35. He said never mind, pay me when you sell them. I did, but it took me two years, during which he never once reminded me of the debt. Sandy is dead now. He was kind to me. Kind men leave a gap when they pass on. The other sort are never missed.

Well, I needn't have worried. Books Two, Three, Four, Five, Six and Seven followed in the next eleven years. All my leisure time was devoted to them. There was never a single free evening when I didn't apply myself to the task with the eagerness of a lover: it was a passionate courtship. I am one of the fortunate men who bungle every household job and so am never asked to tackle anything. Between finishing one book and starting the next, I paused only to refill my pipe.

I was helped at first by Henry Marshall, the Kendal Librarian, who attended to the distribution and despatch of the books. He advised me that it would never do for my name to appear both as author and publisher – a sure indication that no recognised publisher could be persuaded to undertake the responsibility – and so I borrowed his name, which, in any case, had more dignity than mine. I especially liked the Henry. I never disclosed what the Christian A of mine stood for. It suited me to hide the truth of this affliction. But it isn't Aloysius, if that's what you're thinking. Subsequently this arrangement collapsed through weight of numbers. I was having to keep records and do the invoicing and collection as well as write the books, and it was a blessed relief when the Westmorland Gazette of Kendal offered to take over publication in 1963. Henry, too, has passed on, and lies in the little churchyard of Kentmere, amongst the hills.

I came to know every summit, every mountain track and every crag in the district. I never climbed rocks, being too clumsy and imbued with a desire to go on living, but I admired those who did and could well imagine the exhilaration and sense of achievement

*◀ Pavey Ark
across Stickle Tarn*

they must have felt. Jack's Rake and Pavey Ark were my absolute limit. I regarded the rougher mountains with awe and respect and a little fear. That is until I started to venture amongst them on nocturnal outings, climbing in the gathering dusk as the day's walkers were coming down for their suppers, and reaching the tops as daylight drained from the sky and the sheep retired to the beds fashioned for them by their ancestors centuries ago.

On the first few occasions, I carried an Army blanket for warmth, but later discarded it because of its weight and failure to induce sleep. Instead I preferred to find a patch of easy ground and outwit the cold by pacing slowly to and fro across it during the hours of darkness. There was no question of sleep. If you are alone, the experience is eerie. On a still night, the silence is

*Crinkle Crags and Bowfell, with Red Tarn*

▲ *The Scafell range from Hindscarth*   ▼ *Summit of Knott Rigg looking to High Spy*

absolute. There is nothing to see but the black silhouette of the nearby slopes and the skyline and, sometimes, the moon and a million stars. The hours of darkness drag, so I used to spend my time thinking. I lived my life over again. I tried to remember, in sequence, the names of the football teams that had won the Cup in the past ten years. I tried to recall all the women who might have married me if I had asked them, and this passed the time well, not because there were so many but because there were so many doubts about the few. I rationed myself to a cigarette or a pipe every half-hour. I kept trying to kid myself that it was getting lighter, that the dawn was breaking.

An almost imperceptible lightening of the gloom would herald a new day, the higher peaks changed from jet to a ghostly grey or, if the sun had risen above the horizon, to a rosy-pink that slowly travelled downwards to diffuse the shadows of the night. Often the valleys would appear as rivers and lakes of white mist of virgin purity, pierced only by the higher peaks as islands pierce the sea. It was wonderful to witness the mist slowly dissolving in the warmer air and be smiling giants again.

Of course, the dawn might have been grey and damp and I would find that mist had silently shrouded the tops. Even then, the experience was a profound one; it attuned me to the mountains until I felt a part of the living rock; and there was always the company of the sheep. When they resumed their daily business and I could hear cocks crowing down in the valleys, then it was time to be off. Then I had the fells all to myself, for not until midday would the first walkers appear on the scene. I could wander and explore at will undisturbed, visit the summits, make notes and take photographs unobserved. I lost all fear of the fells. Down below I was a pen-pusher. Up here I was a king: a king amongst friends.

Summer and winter, wet or fine, I made weekly expeditions to the fells. On bright clear days I climbed to the summits to note details of the views; on dull or wet days I would check the approaches from the valleys. Never a day was wasted. As at Blackburn, Sundays were different. At Blackburn I had attended chapel. Now I worshipped in nature's cathedrals.

When I had walked all the mountain paths in regular use I sought other routes of ascent to the summits. I liked to climb alongside the becks coming down from the tops, many of them quite unfrequented: they not only set the direction but rewarded

me with vistas of unexpected waterfalls and ravines bedecked *▲ Taking a rest on*
with ferns and flowers, and additionally provided me with liquid *the fells*
refreshment sweeter than nectar. When the streams became a
trickle I continued upwards to reach familiar summits from new
angles. I liked to explore away from the beaten paths, scrambling
over easy rocks and boulders but always careful to leave a line
of retreat if faced by difficulties, in places probably never
seen before. No-man's-lands were my delight. I visited all the
climbers' crags and surveyed them from safe stances below
but the prospect of climbing them turned my legs to jelly; they
were for supermen, not me. With the help of my old set of 1901
Ordnance Survey maps, on a scale of six inches to a mile, I could
follow the forgotten cart-tracks, sledgates and tracks to the old
mines and quarries, long since abandoned.

Two seasons I remember well. In the summer of 1959 I was
engaged on the Scafell group, the highest ground in the district,
and clear weather was necessary for my purpose. Fortune smiled.
Sunday after Sunday I toiled up Rossett Gill to find brilliant
sunshine and perfect visibility on the tops. All through the summer, conditions were exactly right. Too often in Lakeland, summer
haze obscures the views day after day but in 1959 the weekends
were ideal. The Isle of Man was a permanent feature in the view. I
did all I wanted to do and returned to the evening bus at Dungeon
Ghyll a very happy man.

▶ *Eric Beardsall, Peter and AW*

▶ *AW and Peter at the top of Deep Gill, Scafell*

*View north-west from Glaramara*

*Dale Head from High Spy*

*◄ The head of Derwentwater, winter 1963–4*

The other season I recall vividly was the winter of 1963–4. The district was gripped by a severe frost for three months without respite, the lakes were sheets of ice and the fells encased in frozen snow. Whilst the conditions put paid to fellwalking, the scenery of the valleys was very beautiful. Borrowdale, which I visited each Sunday, was transformed into a fairyland of exquisite charm, a delicate tracery of black and white. I was entranced. This was a new Lakeland. Even without colour it was the loveliest place on earth.

I became a creature of habit. I was a regular customer on the 8.30 bus to Keswick every Sunday morning and on the 6.30 back in the evening. Going, I planned the day's walk; returning, I reviewed it. I was known by sight but not by name to some of the other travellers on the bus, to the inspector at Keswick bus station, who thought I was A.H. Griffin and was never contradicted, to a few walkers I met frequently, and at my favourite café in Keswick where I called for a meal before returning home.

My choice of menu never varied. My appearance in the doorway was a signal for Winnie the waitress to call to the kitchen, 'One plaice and chips', this repast being followed by a fruit salad and accompanied by a huge pot of tea which, as I often confirmed, contained enough for ten cups. I remember Winnie's distress when she had to tell me that the price of the meal had been increased from 6s 6d to 7s 6d. Poor Winnie: I heard later that she had died from cancer after a long illness.

Words are inadequate to express and explain the emotional impact the fells had on me. During the making of the books they dominated my thoughts. They held me in chains. The work of the office always came first and I never missed a Council or committee meeting, but the members around the table would have been shocked if they had known that during their earnest deliberations on municipal matters my attention was elsewhere. I was living a double life. I was completely dedicated to the books and spent every available moment on them. The Lakeland garden I had created became an uncharted jungle where the cats of the neighbourhood stalked their prey. Domestic relationships withered and died. The only relaxation I permitted myself was the annual pilgrimage to the Highlands of Scotland, of which more anon.

Perhaps the idea of the books generated first and foremost as a line of escape. Some people escape in dreams but I was fortunate enough to live in a perfect dreamland that actually existed. I was always happier pulling on my boots in a morning than putting on my shoes. On a day when I didn't have to wear a collar and tie I was a boy again. If I was heading for the hills, and not the office, I could set forth singing, not audibly, heaven forbid; just in my heart. I was off to where the sheep were real, not human.

*Upper Eskdale, with the outline of Hardknott Roman Fort showing on the fellside*

*Mickleden seen from Rossett Pike*

# Eight

# ON AND OFF THE FELLS

I was always careful to say that the series would be completed 'all being well', thus insuring myself against any conceivable mishap that might have interrupted the work. I didn't anticipate a loss of interest or enthusiasm: I knew this couldn't happen. What I had in mind was illness, accident, death. Failing eyesight or a tremble in the right hand were also possibilities I feared. Again, I needn't have worried. The precaution was proved unnecessary. I didn't really expect an illness. I have never been ill, nor did I ever miss a minute at work because of sickness during forty-seven years of service. When I reached sixty, my non-walking, car-owning contemporaries were dropping like flies, but I remained immune from any ailment, and this may be no coincidence. Walking is almost the only exercise that a man can indulge without loss of facility from childhood to the grave. It is a natural function of the body to walk, it isn't to drive a car . . .

Accidents on the fells should never happen to walkers. They do happen, though, but only as the result of clumsiness or a lack of ordinary common sense, never from circumstances beyond their control. It amuses me to see all the articles and treatises and even books written on the subject of walking on the fells. Goodness me, if a person needs a manual of instruction on walking he should stay at home. Walking is one of the first things we learn. Our mothers taught us, remember? We do it all our lives. In a city street it's a matter of staying balanced on the feet while moving forward, just as we were taught as children. On a fell it's a matter of staying balanced on the feet while moving forward, just as we were taught as children. What else is there to learn? Nothing. But, unfortunately, fellwalking accidents are good news for the papers. Sprain an ankle on Esk Hause and be helped down, and you are headlines. Sprain an ankle in Market Street and be helped home, and who

*Scafell Crag and Mickledore*

*Crummock Water and the Loweswater Valley from Lad Hows*

▲ *Grasmere with Seat Sandal behind*

cares? Fellwalking is not a dangerous sport. It is not a sport at all. It is a pleasure. If you don't find it a pleasure, don't bother to do it and don't expect to make it a pleasure by reading a textbook. Those who utter grave warnings about it annoy me: they are doing a disservice. Fellwalking isn't dicing with death: it is a glorious enjoyment of life.

Fellwalking accidents happen only to those who walk clumsily. The only advice you need (and this shouldn't be necessary either) is to watch where you are putting your feet. Do this and you will not have an accident. In fact, fellwalking brings immunity against accidents. It is a wonderful exercise, the best of all. It strengthens the legs, clears the mind, and tones up the whole body to a state of exhilaration: you can't get these benefits through the Welfare State, nor from a doctor, nor from pills. Essentially, fellwalking means rough walking and it strengthens the ankles. Unlike road walking, where the feet are put down in exactly the same fashion for mile after mile, on the fells the feet are rarely put down exactly the same for two steps together. There are stony paths and bare rock, boulders and bogs, smooth grass and tussocky clumps, streams and peat-hags, all to be negotiated in the course of a mountain walk, and rarely is one step like the next. All the muscles in the foot, ankle and leg are continuously exercised, not monotonously as in a road walk but in refreshing variety. The last things to tire on rough terrain are the feet, the first things on a tarmac road are the feet. Almost all accidents occur in descent, not in ascent, and they should never happen in descent, either. They don't with experience. But the novice usually expects danger in going uphill, perhaps because mountain climbing is associated with moving upwards, but you can't go up without coming down. It is wrong to think that the risk of accident is over when the top is reached; it isn't, it's only just starting. The secret, and it isn't really a secret at all because it becomes second nature with a little experience, is to keep the feet horizontal or even pointing slightly upwards when descending, and don't point them down the slope; keeping them horizontal means taking advantage of protruding stones and tufts of grass and flat ledges, and after a season or two one does this instinctively and automatically, without thinking. Every step downwards should be planned to act as a brake. The eye is a stride ahead of the foot all the time. Watch where you are putting your feet, every step. Come down the Breast Route on Great Gable with the feet horizontal and you will not slip; come down with the feet pointing down the slope and much of the journey

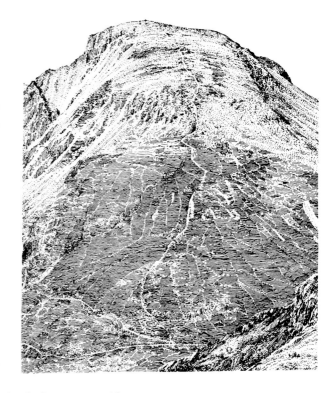

▲ *Great Gable*

will be done sliding on your back. And always *stop* if you want to look at the view. Don't think you can come down the Breast Route and admire the Scafells simultaneously. For the third time, watch where you are putting your feet!

As for common sense: well, some people haven't the sense they were born with. There is no hope for such folk and they should not go on the hills at all. They invite a broken leg by jumping from boulder to boulder; they expect providence to deliver them safely if they step over the edge of a cliff, whereas providence is simply fed up with them, and won't; they wander like lost souls in mist and get into places where they can neither proceed further nor turn back, not thinking, as anyone with ordinary sense would, to leave an easy line of retreat behind them. You can't learn common sense from a book, either.

People who go for a walk on the fells are often strongly advised to leave details of the route they intend to follow. The idea, presumably, is that when they break their several legs, the lads from Keswick and Langdale and Coniston and other places who form the rescue teams will know where to go to look for them. Forget about this miserable and misleading association of

*The Scafells from Middle Fell*

*Borrowdale from the slopes of Brund Fell*

*▲ AW relaxing with friends, having achieved the summit*

fellwalking and accidents! Would these advisers exempt Pearson Dalton, the lone shepherd of Skiddaw House? Poor Pearson must do his daily rounds but has nobody to tell where he is going, and he only goes home at weekends: he little realises his life is in jeopardy every time he sets out! The advice may be all right for youngsters, but it is tyranny for an experienced walker to have to tell anyone where he is going if he doesn't want to. The whole essence of fellwalking – and for this we should thank the land-owners and the tenant farmers and the National Trust – is free-dom to wander along the paths on the fells, and freedom to plan a route as you go along, and free-dom to change your mind. The hills are not death-traps, but invigorating playgrounds, places for exercise and the study of geology and botany and wild life. You don't go on the hills to break your neck. You go on the hills to get away from places where other people can break your neck. When you step off the tarmac on to the rough ground, danger is past, not just beginning. If a man arrives at Sty Head and likes the look of the Corridor Route more than the Breast Route up Great Gable, he ought to take the Corridor Route and not have it on his conscience that he told the old johnny with the bald head over the breakfast table that he would be doing Great Gable from Sty Head that day. If, when he arrives at Sty Head, the cool waters of the tarn appeal more as the day's ultimate objective than the dusty screes of Great Gable, he ought not to feel he is not playing the game as he swims around in the sunshine: he is. If, when he arrives at Sty Head, the weather has improved so much that he wishes to change his plans completely and traverse the Glaramara ridge instead, he ought to be able to do so with no doubts in his mind. All he needs in his mind is to remember to watch where he is putting his feet and to use his common sense.

Solitary fellwalking is often roundly condemned, not by solitary fellwalkers but by non-solitary fellwalkers and non-fellwalkers including coroners. Always walk with others, they say. This is excellent advice for those who lack ordinary gumption, or are plain daft; and such people, if they go on the fells at all, which they shouldn't, can be further advised to get themselves in the middle of a big party and keep themselves hemmed in by the sweating flesh of others. At the end of the day, they won't know where they've been and they won't have seen much, but at any rate they won't have been lost or killed themselves: they'll be proud of this, and it is not for us to reason why.

It might be good advice for those who are new to the hills until they get the feel of the high places. But to a careful and experienced fellwalker the advice is intolerable. It is the man or woman who walks alone who enjoys the greatest rewards, who sees and feels and senses the mood of the hills and knows them most intimately, and it is no coincidence that they are people of abundant common sense and initiative and imagination. To the man in a conducted party the mountains are prose, to the man travelling alone they are poetry. Of course he has nobody to talk to, which is an advantage, and there is nobody to talk to him, which is a bigger advantage; he has nothing to distract his attention and nobody to consult or argue with, he goes where his nose leads him, makes his own pace, halts when and where he likes, responds to nature's demands on the spot without redfaced apologies. Absolute freedom includes freedom from the presence of others. Some people (in parties) pity the solitary walker, and seem unable to understand that he walks alone by preference. But surely a man doesn't have to be odd to enjoy his own company best, once in a while; away from the hills he has precious few opportunities for quiet meditation. And if a man cannot enjoy his own company, what effect does he think it has on others? Sometimes the reverse is the case: I always consider myself, when alone, a vastly entertaining companion, but when with others am considered unsociable, boorish, not with it.

Again, some people (in parties) confuse aloneness with loneliness, but there is all the difference in the world between being alone and being lonely. I was least lonely when I was alone on the hills and free to indulge my imagination; most lonely in a crowd. The worst experience that befalls a solitary walker is coming face to face with a large party, especially when they are strung out

*Scafell Pike and Ill Crag from Throstle Garth*

▲ *Sheffield Pike above the valley of Glencoyne*   ▼ *Seatoller at the foot of Honister Pass*

along his path. In a tight place, where this many-headed and many-legged caterpillar cannot be bypassed, it must be confronted. It may be a party of thirty-six. Every one of them ventures a greeting of sorts (the courtesy code of the hills, y'know). If I were in sociable mood I would mumble a response to the first. The rest had to share it. I was not going to say good afternoon thirty-six times in quick succession. The tail-end probably thought me a surly beggar. Okay, so I did not like large parties on the hills. Large groups spoil the paths. They leave litter. They get under the feet. Half of them always seem to be on the point of dropping dead. Many are obviously not enjoying themselves, and should not be there at all. Leave the hills to those who most appreciate them is my motto.

I mentioned mist. Nothing is more terrifying to the uninitiated. In their minds, tormented by grim warnings, mist is associated with getting lost, with walking in circles, with fatal accidents. It is true that one tends to walk in circles, clockwise, in country that lacks distinctive features. I remember once walking up the path from Wrynose Pass to Red Tarn and leaving it to make the short, untracked beeline to the top of Cold Pike: the ground at first is

▼ *High Pike from High Sweden Bridge*

fairly flat, with grassy swells. Everything was hidden in mist. After twenty minutes I found myself on a good path, which I knew shouldn't be there. It was the path I had left, a hundred yards further on. I set off again in the right direction but after a further twenty minutes found myself back on the same path once more, after which I abandoned Cold Pike and let the path take me down into Langdale. Walking in circles is amusing and interesting, but not frightening. Getting lost shouldn't happen.

There are two kinds of mist on the hills, never fog. There is dry mist, which floats around the fellsides like a gossamer veil, always mobile but clinging to the gullies and hollows: it drifts silently across the scene, one moment impenetrable, the next torn into windows that give exquisite glimpses of the far distance in a white surround, the next vanished completely. Of all weather conditions on the fells, the most fascinating is dry mist. There is no venom in it, only a playful mischief. More than

*◄ Dollywaggon Pike across Grisedale Pass*

anything, mist expresses the atmosphere of the mountains. Mountains generate mist and look naked without their delicate white shawls. The effects are often startling, often incredibly beautiful, always interesting, never frightening.

But the other sort of mist is wet mist, hanging immovably over the tops, its lower limit a horizontal line as straight as though drawn with a ruler. This is cloud, charged with raindrops, and causing saturation as surely as a torrential downpour; there is no pleasure in such conditions, and those who walk for pleasure, as all should, give the tops a miss on such days. Mist is never so thick that one cannot see one's hands in front of one's face, and those who claim to have experienced mist like this are telling fibs. In the thickest mist or cloud, visibility is never down to less than ten yards in the hours of daylight, enough to follow a beaten track, and it is to defeat these conditions that the lines of cairns have been erected to indicate the most frequented routes. Then the cairns become friendly guides and many a lost soul has had occasion to bless them with the fervour of a Tibetan pilgrim reaching a prayer-shrine. Dry mist is a charmer, wet mist a snare, but neither is the cause of accidents, but clumsy walking is.

*Pikes Crag and Hollow Stones, Scafell*

*Wastwater Screes*

If clumsy walkers did no more than damage themselves they would be welcome to go on doing it, but they also spoil the paths for everybody else. Bulls in china shops are gentle creatures compared with some of the pedestrians one sees, and hears, in Rossett Gill or Little Hell Gate. They are often verbally noisy, a common characteristic of the insensitive, but it is their boots that cause most clatter. Flying stones, uprooted sods, and blasphemous shouts accompany their sliding progress, especially downhill, in a surround of noise. At home, one imagines, there will not be a cup with a handle, not a chair without broken springs, not a door with a knob left on. But a good walker moves silently and is a joy to behold. He moves not gracefully, but rhythmically. His footstep is firm. He presses the path into place with his boots, and improves it. The clumsy walker loosens and destroys paths. A good walker loves the zigzags of a path, which always give the easiest progression, but a bad walker can't be bothered, cuts across them and ruins them for others. A good walker always gives the impression of moving leisurely, even slowly, and having time to spare; a bad walker always seems to be in a hurry. A good walker will climb Scafell Pike from Sty Head and hardly disturb a single stone; a bad walker will leave a trail of debris. Their respective journeys through life will be the same.

I have mentioned boots, and might borrow Kipling's song title to emphasise the word thrice, because boots are the best footgear for the hills. But wear shoes or sandals or go barefoot if any of these suit you better. Reams have been written on what to wear on the hills, but ignore such advice. The thing is to wear what is most comfortable for you. It is a matter of individual choice; don't be dictated to. Clothes never become comfortable until they are shabby and shapeless and well perforated by sparks from the pipe – at least, mine don't – and when you can no longer appear at the office in them without shame they are ready to serve you on the hills, where nobody is there to see them and wouldn't bother if they did. Comfort is the thing. Comfort includes keeping warm and dry, but ways of achieving it differ widely. The most ghastly apparitions appear on the fells, spectral creatures and scarecrows on two legs, representing varying conceptions of the ideal mountain garb. If sheep didn't have such good manners they would laugh their heads off. Clothing is an individual matter. You don't have to look like the man in front. As with everything else, one learns from experience.

A lot of advice has been given by various authorities on equipment: the need for taking a map and compass and a whistle (they never mention guidebooks, drat them!), on stoves and cooking gear, on exposure meters and lenses and filters and so on. And a lot of rot has been said. Well, please yourself if you want to carry a load of hardware and ironmongery around, but don't make fellwalking a game to be played by rules. It is a pleasure, as I have said, or it is not fellwalking at all. It is something to enjoy or something to endure: it cannot be both. You see hikers setting forth for a day on the hills burdened as though they were starting a six-month expedition to Antarctica: they are grim and anguished of face when they ought to be carefree and smiling. They are not going into uncharted wastes and should have no more sense of apprehension or impending risk than if they were going for a Sunday afternoon stroll in the park. The hills are friendly: there are no lurking hazards. The dangers have been absurdly exaggerated; you are not making a date with death, you are not making a technical excursion into space. You are going for a walk, that's all, no different from all other walks except that there is more up and down and the way is likely to be rougher, and you are going to see and enjoy beautiful scenery, wild and lonely places and visions of loveliness that will bring tears to your eyes and joy to your heart at the same time; but you are far more likely to run into danger crossing the main street of Keswick. If you get into trouble on the fells it will be your own fault; in the main street of Keswick it might not be. The fells are not monsters, but amiable giants. You can romp over them and pull the hairs on their chests and shout in their ears and treat them rough, and they don't mind a bit. They are not enemies to be wrestled with. They are friends. Go amongst them as you go amongst friends.

▲ *Dash Falls near Skiddaw*

▲ *Skiddaw from Baggra Yeat*   ▼ *Skiddaw and the Vale of Keswick from Catbells*

*Long Side and Ullock Pike*

For me, a map and a camera were enough: the map to look at now and then and to study if I had to spend an hour under a boulder out of the rain; and the camera for recording permanently the transient, often fleeting, beauty of a landscape caressed by sun and shadow. I never carried a compass, preferring to rely on a good sense of direction, and in my case the latter always proved reliable, more than a compass could ever be and certainly less fiddly to consult. But all authorities insist that a compass should be taken, so perhaps you should. In my case, I didn't because I never bothered to understand how a compass works or what it is supposed to do. To me, a compass is a gadget, and I don't get on well with gadgets of any sort. They never seem to work for me as they do for other people.

My mind is full of dreams and imaginings and romance, and is strictly non-technical. The fells are honest and have no gadgets. Anything operated by a mechanism is miles over my head. Wheels and switches and levers and things belong to another world, not mine. I have tried hard to understand, heaven knows. I have studied simple mechanisms intently for hours. But they will not work for me. I could never solve bent-nail puzzles or unravel knots. You cannot appreciate the awful and utter loneliness of a man who does not understand gadgets in a world that is becoming full of them, and in a life that cannot be lived without them. People who ask me why I haven't a motor car are turning a knife in my heart. But I have found that there is always somebody who knows and is ready to come to the rescue, somebody who will pityingly and patronisingly offer to do it for me. In fact, it's not at all bad not being able to do things. Other people do them for you, not really out of kindness but because they like to demonstrate their superior intellect. You get your knots unravelled: you get your jobs done for you. You get free rides in motor cars, and admire the passing scenery while other people drive and get their hands dirty and pay the petrol bills. You remain an innocent in these matters.

Cameras have gadgets, of course. Mine is a second-hand one, a simple one with various contrivances such as range-finder, flash-bulb and self-portrait device, but I don't know which is which or what they are supposed to do, so I leave them alone. I can take a used film out and put a new one in, and know which knob to press to take a picture (my son showed me when he was very young) but the rest is a closed book I have never been able

*◄ Sadgill,*
*Longsleddale*

to open. I have the same trouble with gates. Gates are gadgets to
close an opening in a wall or fence. Hundreds of them are
encountered in the intakes and on the lower slopes, but there seem
to be as many ways of fastening a gate as there are gates. No two
are quite alike. With some of them you can't tell which end is
supposed to open. A good tip is first to determine which end has
the hinges: in theory, it is the other end that opens, or should. My
heart dropped when I saw them across my path. They meant
confusion and delay. I spent hours every year trying to open
gates. A few were obvious and simple, but many were too
ingenious for me. Some couldn't be made to open at all. Then
they had to be climbed, and nine times out of ten the same thing
happened. You would get one foot on the bottom rung, which
stayed firm until your other leg was at its maximum height when
being thrown over the other side, whereupon it would collapse
and so did you upon the top rung, cruelly impaling delicate
organs of the body thereon. My, how it hurt! Sometimes the pain
creased you for the rest of the day. Perhaps I should have
recounted this latter experience in the first person, not knowing
how women fare when bisected in this fashion. In fact, I suffered

*Skiddaw from Friar's Crag, Derwentwater*

*▲ Blencathra and Clough Head from Causey Pike   ▼ Blencathra from Maiden Moor*

quite a bit during the making of those guidebooks. But never as the result of a walking accident – I always watched where I was putting my feet. It's the man-made gadgets that defeat and destroy me.

Returning to the subject of cameras, I must be modest as befits my amateur status as a photographer. I don't profess to know much about lenses and shutters and related contrivances, and never had, or wanted, an exposure meter, which always sounds to me rather indecent. I have an eye for a good subject, but trust to luck in capturing it. I get the oddest results. Some pictures that should be absolute winners turn out to be grey and drab and worthless; some despairing snaps turn out better than expected. I must have taken thousands of pictures on my walks. Most were adequate for my purpose, to record some detail, but just occasionally, and often enough by mischance, there is a good one in the batch just back from being developed. Out of thousands, some are bound to be up to standard. The photographs in this book are my best, and they are the real justification for the book.

I had the title for my book, *Fellwanderer*, before the contents. I liked it, although it suggested an autobiography, which is the next to the last thing I would ever dream of doing. *Fellwandering* would perhaps overcome this difficulty, but in turn suggested a manual of walking instruction, which is positively the last thing I would ever dream of doing, believing such a book to be quite unnecessary except for half-wits. The readers of my guidebooks are not half-wits. They are people of exceptional charm and intelligence and enthusiasm for the fells. Not the least of my rewards has been a constant stream of appreciative letters from all manner of folk and from all sorts of unlikely places. Some were straightforward enquiries about accommodation and itineraries and mountain campsites and the like, and some simply recounted personal experiences and adventures. But a thousand I have kept, and I count them a thousand treasures. People have been very kind, and many letters have been quite touching, the sort that humble a man and shame his conceit. Some were from lame or infirm people, who had found a few of the easier climbs within their powers and wrote to express their joy for experiences they thought they could never share with the more fortunate. Some were from people in hospital beds, who had wondered what the mountains of Lakeland were really like, and now felt they knew; some were from

people beset by worry and anxiety who had turned to the hills for ▲ *Great Slab,* the first time and there found the solace they needed, and had *Bowfell* since become regular visitors; some were from elderly people who had long looked at the fells but never dared to venture upon them until they were given confidence; some were from servicemen in far-off countries who yearned for the hills of their homeland; some were from exiles born in the shadow of the fells who had never forgotten or ceased to love them; some contained generous offers of hospitality in the remoter districts, or the use of cars and services as chauffeurs. Many were from fathers and mothers who had been encouraged to take their children on the tops and by doing so had transformed their family life and forged new bonds between themselves.

And many, a great many, were from the children themselves, telling of their wonderful adventures in simple words that are often the most effective. Do take the children on the hills early, in a rucksack on your shoulders if they can't yet walk. Children are born scramblers and don't hurt easily: it's yourself you want to watch, not them. They will be in a seventh heaven of delight. They don't fear the elements or the mountains. Fear only comes

▲ *Blea Crag, High Spy, looking to Helvellyn*   ▼ *The Buttermere Valley*

▲ *Crummock Water*   ▼ *The Buttermere Valley from Kirkstile*

with age. It always pleases me to see a family party on a mountain track. There, I think, goes a good father and an even better mother. They have the right idea. They want their children to know and love the quiet places before the noisy world offers less desirable outlets for juvenile enthusiasm and energy and enterprise. A child forgets many incidents of childhood, but he will always remember the day his old dad took him along the Climbers Traverse on Bowfell and up the Great Slab. There are red-letter days in infancy, too.

Yes, all my correspondents were kind. I tried to acknowledge all letters, but could do so only briefly, and too often after unseemly delay. I used to build up a cairn of unanswered letters on my desk, and still do, and when it collapsed reply to a few and build up the rest again. There really hasn't been time to give them the attention they deserved, and I'm sorry. People have told me their difficulties and troubles, too, but never once in a complaining fashion, and I have marvelled at their fortitude and resolve. Now with my own eyesight failing, I realise that while we are fit and well and able to enjoy life fully, we ought to count our blessings more. Then we are the fortunate ones. It makes for humility to read of others counting their blessings who have far fewer to count. Those of us who have most cause to do it, rarely trouble. We take things for granted far too much these days. We who have the best reason to be satisfied are often the least satisfied. We grab for more when we have enough already.

▼ *The summit cairn on Great End*

Writers of guidebooks always strive to get their facts right, knowing there will be reprimands if they don't. I have often travelled a hundred miles merely to check the existence or position of a particular wall or sheepfold, or to verify a small detail that was not clear in my mind, or to be absolutely sure that a certain mountain can be seen from a certain other. But the way of the perfectionist is hard. Facts don't stay right. The letters come in. 'Dear Mr. Wainwright, you omitted to indicate a

stile . . .' I didn't. It's been put up since. 'Why didn't you show this path? . . .' Because there wasn't any path when I was there in 1956. 'You showed a signpost and there isn't one . . .' You're dead right, mate, somebody took it for firewood. In Book Seven, I drew particular attention to the new stretcher-box on Shamrock Traverse, describing it as a useful landmark to guide walkers across a rough section of country. After the book was printed but not yet published, I read with dismay that the box had disintegrated because of frost, and knew that unless the Cockermouth Rescue Team rescued my reputation by replacing it I should have more puzzled correspondents to pacify. Guidebooks are quickly out of date, some even, as in this instance, before they leave the printers. Some facts stay right. Seven times four is always twenty-eight. I would have enjoyed a greater peace of mind if I

▲ *The packhorse bridge at Low Hartsop*   ▼ *Stockley Bridge in Borrowdale*

▲ *Blencathra seen from Castlerigg Stone Circle*    ▼ *Swinside Stone Circle*

had published a book of multiplication tables. Or would I? On reflection, no, I wouldn't, of course not. Peace of mind comes to me on the hills. The changes that take place are trivial, merely a plucking of little threads in the tremendous backcloth of the mountain scene, and of no consequence in the general pattern. Mickledore will be just the same in a thousand years, Sharp Edge no less sharp, Sty Head no less exciting. The hills will always be there, always giving peace of mind.

Some readers have helped me by drawing my attention to certain features they thought worth mentioning. Molly Lefebure was one who did her best to help. She tried. She told me of a stone circle she had discovered on Burnbank Fell during a fox-hunt. I must not mention the circumstances that led to its discovery, but I kept the antiquity in mind as 'Molly's Shame' until I visited the area. But could I, then, find a stone circle on Burnbank Fell? No, I couldn't. I spent a month of Saturdays crawling around Burnbank Fell almost on hands and knees in a vain search for it, at first eagerly, but latterly as a man without hope. 'Molly's Shame' became 'Molly's Folly'. I climbed walls and fences, not heeding discomfort, as though seeking the Holy Grail. The reward – nothing. The cost – a great hole torn in my trousers by barbed wire, and in such a vital place that I had to partake of tea at a Loweswater hotel with legs tightly crossed, and wear my plastic mac all the way home although the day was sunny and warm. I gave up after that.

I wrote to the lady, gently: 'There is *no* stone circle on Burnbank Fell, love. The village lads must have been larking about.' Stung to the quick, she set out to prove me wrong. Let me quote from her next letter: 'Well, to tell you the ghastly truth, I have made one or two little sorties there myself recently and found – nothing. But you must believe that I did originally find a circle. And as proof of my perfect conviction of this circle let me tell you that I, when I first went back, proceeded straight to where I believed this circle to be: I went straight to it like a wretched homing pigeon. I was alone, but if I had had you or anyone else with me, such a companion would have noticed how I went to the presumed place without a second's hesitation. It was a real blow when there was no circle! These preliminary fruitless trips unsettled me: still, it is easy to mistake a place on a fellside. Then came your cry that you were giving up the search, and that there was, or is, no circle.

'Well, on Tuesday I went once again to Burnbank Fell with some German friends who have been staying here, and an assortment of children. This was to be the final expedition to end all expeditions and, since I believed I would ultimately find the circle (in spite of all you said), I took a camera, a notebook, a compass, a pencil or two, and a metal measuring rod thing that flips back into a metal spool, weighs very heavy and is extremely dangerous: have your finger off in no time if you relaxed your guard for an instant. This scientific equipment was designed to record the indisputable evidence of a circle, with which evidence A.W. was going to be crushed.

'The search party was scientifically lined up, each person taking a contour, and off we went: very slowly, inch by inch examining the ground. This went on all day, the search in final desperation being extended to Mockerkin How. We found four dead sheep, a lot of mosquitoes and an abominable species of particularly brutal thistle that gave me such a jab in the leg that I thought for one panic-stricken moment that I had been bitten by an adder, and I was about to start screaming and demanding to be rushed to hospital for snake-bite serum when fortunately I noticed the thistle. This was a blessing, for everybody was already looking at me askance because of getting them all out there in that place of desolation on such a beautiful day when we could have been by Crummock Water. An imaginary stone circle was bad enough, an imaginary snake into the bargain would have been the final straw.

'The search was prolonged and resulted in nothing but the Aga being out when we got home and dinner arriving on the table, in consequence, at the hour of twenty minutes to twelve, midnight. It was a delicious dinner, and gaiety abounded, the hostess being particularly lively – but with a heavy load lurking in the secret recesses of her heart. For, to tell you the truth, I am now of the opinion myself that there is no longer a stone circle on Burnbank Fell, Mr Wainwright darling. I cannot possibly think what can have happened to it; that I found it I have no doubt. It was there, exact and perfect and melancholy and deserted, and indeed should be known not as my Shame nor a Folly but as Molly's Magic Circle.'

And here is a bitter extract from mine, in reply: 'The Franco-German sweep across the flanks of Burnbank Fell deserved the wide canvas of a Cecil B. de Mille spectacular. The march of Lefebure and her forces across those barren wastes was epic stuff,

*The summit of Harter Fell, looking to the Scafells*

*The Scafells from Crinkle Crags*

the best thing since Moses or somebody led the children of Israel across the desert. Never was an operation more carefully planned, never were troops more skilfully deployed, never was a crusade more sure of success. The battle orders were simple: search for a stone circle marked LADIES. But as the hours passed, as the sun wheeled across the sky, as Lefebure hoarsely urged on her faltering legions throughout the long day until they were no more than black silhouettes against the darkening gloom, as, finally, the disorganised and despondent rabble, crushed to defeat and near to rebellion, trailed in disarray back o'er the hills whence they came, then the star of Wainwright shone brightly over the deserted moor.' I keep telling Molly our letters to each other (suitably edited) should be published: they would bring the house down.

I could have written a better book if I had some personal adventures to recount. But I haven't, none worth the telling. The thirteen years during which I produced the Seven Pictorial Guides were a dreamlike procession of happy uneventful days. The minor disappointments of climbing a fell to note the view and then finding the top shrouded in mist, or having to come down

▼ *Pillar from Great Gable*

prematurely to catch a bus, or getting soaked with nothing to show for it, were soon forgotten. I always got a walk anyway, and a good tea. I never had an accident, or a fall, I was never benighted in a blizzard or tossed by a bull. I always walked alone – by preference. I would have been poor company, anyway. I had work to do – maps to check, details of ascents to note, photographs to take, views to record – and I could not afford any distractions. Furthermore, I had this work to do unseen or at least unnoticed by others. If there's one thing I cannot stand, it's someone looking over my shoulder. If there's another, it's someone asking silly questions. If there's another, it's being pointed out. I suffer fools badly.

*▲ Haystacks and Scarth Gap from Gamlin End*

So I had to be anonymous, and what a furtive character I became! It was funny really. My general appearance was fairly well known among walkers, due to some unwelcome publicity. My height and size I couldn't disguise. If I discarded my spectacles I would have fallen over a cliff. Harry Griffin had described me in one of his books as rather distinguished looking, which pleased me on the whole although I never quite forgave him the qualifying adjective. Older readers will remember that there used

*Grasmoor and Rannerdale Knotts across Crummock Water*

*Hobcarton Crag, Hopegill Head, from Grisedale Pike*

to be a character known as Lobby Lud, and if you spotted him amongst the seaside crowds you were given a reward; £5, I think. It was a newspaper stunt. Well, I became another Lobby Lud, but I didn't hand out rewards. I knew many people were on the lookout for me: they had told me so by letter. They knew approximately where I was operating, or at least they knew the area I was working on. Yes, I was furtive all right. I liked a fell to myself, and particularly a summit. I often found these conditions, especially in the remoter and little-known districts, and here I was really happy and could work undisturbed. On the more popular fells I had to observe many subterfuges to keep out of other people's way. If a summit was already occupied upon arrival, I had to hang about in the vicinity until it was vacated. If others were coming along my path I wandered off it a while, behind a wall or a boulder, to avoid conversation. I have no doubt at all that those who were bypassed thus thought I had detoured to obey a call; the same call, incidentally, I can claim to have obeyed on every square mile of Lakeland and with special satisfaction in Manchester's gathering grounds. I was not always successful, I mean in avoiding people, and the inevitable happened on a few occasions. I kept hearing stories of other solitary walkers who may have borne some resemblance, poor lads, who were having a rough time of it ('Mr Wainwright, I presume?') but I did pretty well myself. If challenged, my answer depended on the circumstances obtaining at the time and on the age and particularly the sex of the questioner. Yes, I made the acquaintance of some nice ladies. There was one, however, to whom I owe a profound apology, and I had better get it off my conscience now, because she will certainly read this book and recognise herself.

It happened on the summit of High Stile on a glorious Sunday afternoon, 26 July 1964. She was seated by the cairn and was accompanied by a small boy; they had apparently come up from Buttermere. I was in a desperate hurry to catch a bus at Ennerdale Bridge, there was no time to wait for her to depart, and conditions were ideal for two photographs I needed to complete my panorama from the summit. I sat down a few yards away and got my pictures. She approached me and asked, 'Are you Mr Wainwright?' 'No,' I said. 'Well,' she said, 'I know what he looks like and you look like him and I know he's working in this area at present; I do so want to meet him.' I was a bit sorry then; my chances with the ladies were few and far between, but there was

that confounded bus and the cock had already crowed once. 'No,'
I said again, 'but I know who you mean.' Then off I went, and
looking back saw her leave the summit. I'm sorry, lass, whoever
you are.

There were others to whom I said yes, others to whom I said
no. People in parties always got a no. I adopted the name of A.
Walker, which I thought very clever. The A here can stand for
Aloysius, if you want.

One of the best ways to avoid other people was, as I have already
described, by climbing to the tops at dusk, and spending the night
there. Once you have spent a night on a mountain, you are never
again awed by it but think of it with affection. The best bivouac I
ever had was on Harrison Stickle. The evening was fine and I was
in position before dark, near the headwaters of Dungeon Ghyll.

During the hours of darkness a thin drizzle set in. An insidious
wet veil was drawn across the fell and stayed until just before
daylight, when it cleared. When a reluctant dawn lightened the
sky I took the opportunity to exercise my legs and climbed up to
the cairn overlooking Langdale. The scene I saw then was the
most beautiful I have ever witnessed. The tops were clear,
although stark and sullen in the half-light, but below me the
valley was completely filled by a white mist that extended from
the steep upthrust of Rossett Pike at the dalehead and curved like
an unbroken glacier, following the contours of the valley away
into the distance over Elterwater and above the length of Windermere to the sea, a river of vapour, a mantle of unblemished
purity. It was enough to make a man weep. There was complete
stillness in the air and a profound silence over all. Far below,
somewhere beneath the ceiling of mist, I could hear the cocks
crowing. There were people in their beds down there who knew
nothing of the glory of the morning. I stayed until the sun rose
and coloured the peaks in a soft glow. Then there was movement,
the mist gradually breaking up and revealing the patchwork of
fields in the valley, and in a few minutes only a few white
puffballs floated in the still air. It was time to be off. The sheep
had already left their couches among the boulders and were
patiently and perseveringly foraging, as they would do without
intermission until another dusk ended another day. Completely
contented, and having amazing fortitude, the sheep are the truest
lovers of the high places. Come rain, come wind, they are happy

*▶ Langdale Pikes from Side Pike*

with little. Unlike man, often miserable with much, they never complain.

It was during my lonely wanderings on the mountains that I developed an admiration for the birds and animals who shared my days: the sheep, the fell ponies, the occasional foxes and deer, the ravens, the hawks, the buzzards and, in later years, the Mardale eagles. I admired them for their uncomplaining acceptance of the harsh conditions in which they lived, for their independence. They are content with little, wanting only to be left in peace.

During the night I spent on Harrison Stickle I was, for a time before darkness, privileged to watch a fox on a grassy shelf below me, obviously enjoying life, playing alone like a kitten, rolling around on its back like a dog; and not for the first time I fell to wondering whether foxhunting was a cruel sport that should be stopped. Those who practise it say it isn't, that the fox has a fair chance of escape and will escape if it is clever enough, and that, if caught, the end is sudden and merciful. All this is true, but they go too far if they say that the fox actually enjoys being hunted. Only a fox knows this and no fox ever said so. It may, until the awful moment of realisation that there is not going to be any

*The Newlands Pass and Robinson*

*Newlands Valley looking to Blencathra from Robinson*

escape this time, that the enemy has won, that the snapping jaws of the hounds can no longer be avoided: there is no enjoyment then, but terror. Yet this, after all, is nature's way. The buzzard swoops on the vole, the cat on the mouse. It is better than man's way, with guns or poisons.

The dalesmen think so, too. I remember walking up out of Longsleddale one morning and coming across a shepherd leaning on a gate just below Wren Quarry. He asked me whether I had seen any men with guns down in the valley. I said I had, and then he told me that he had heard a whisper that a fox-shoot had been arranged for that day, on Harter Fell, and that he had forestalled it by going up on the fell early with his dogs and driving the foxes away over the other side of Mardale: they'll be wasting their time, he said with satisfaction. This man told me of foxes he had seen crippled by gunshot, painfully dying a slow death because they could no longer search for food, and he himself had no doubt that hunting with hounds was the only merciful way of keeping the numbers under control.

But it's a beastly business, this slaughter of animals. Their greatest enemy is man, sharing the same world but refusing to acknowledge that these creatures are neighbours with equal rights to existence. It is a shocking indictment of the human race that wild animals and birds flee in fear at the approach of man who, endowed with superior intellect, abuses this gift by treating all other creatures as objects to be exploited as he wishes for his own benefit. Man is the bully, the biggest and cruellest predator of all. I lost my faith in the human race when the loathsome disease of myxomatosis was deliberately introduced to rid the country of its innocent rabbits, condemning them to a painful and lingering death, and doing so without shame. There are guilty men who go out with guns and traps to shoot and capture their harmless victims and think it great fun: sport, they call it; I rejoice when I hear of a gun going off accidentally and wounding or killing a so-called sportsman. And the catalogue of crime continues to grow. New acts of cruelty to birds and animals have been devised in recent years with official approval. The gassing of badgers was carried out on Government instructions (and admitted later to have been a mistake). The clubbing of seals and the killing of other species to provide fur coats for uncaring women is reprehensible and so are those who wear them. Factory farming, the practice of confining birds and animals in cages and pens

*Robinson from Scope End*

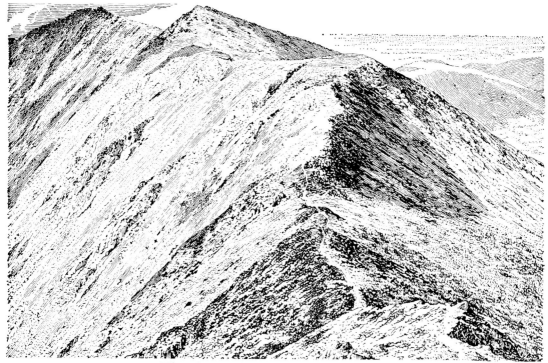

*The ridge to Whiteside from Hopegill Head*

that allow no freedom of movement, meets only feeble protests that carry no weight; I would like to see the farmers who subject living creatures to such torture for monetary gain put in cages three feet square themselves and fed through a grill until they repent their evil methods: a punishment to fit the crime. We have got it wrong when we refer to animals as beasts; the beasts in this world are human beings.

Worse still is vivisection, the cutting up and mistreatment by torture of animals in the cause of medical research, allegedly to find cures for human ailments: human ailments, mind you, not animal ailments. Surely it stands to sense that if these experiments are necessary they should be conducted on humans; of course there would be no volunteers; people, unlike animals, can say no. Yet our prisons are full of murderers and terrorists and rapists and muggers who could be used instead of being kept in comfort at the expense of others. But no, our medical laboratories and even our universities, the seats of learning, prefer defenceless animals as subjects for their barbarism. Anything likely to injure humanity, such as nuclear bombs, causes an outcry and demonstrations but there is little feeling for the suffering of animals deliberately caused. We fear for our own skins and ours only. Millions of animals, to whom life is equally precious, are forced to undergo cruel experiments every year, and nobody in authority turns a hair. The general apathy of the public towards domestic animals is also appalling. Dogs are thrown out of cars on motorways, kittens dumped in plastic bags on rubbish tips, and few care. The church, professing concern for all God's creatures, does nothing.

The human race has nothing to be proud of in its treatment of fellow creatures unable to protect or defend themselves, nothing at all. We are guilty and stand condemned. We should hang our heads in shame. But we don't.

At the time I was completing the guidebooks, I had no idea that, many years later, I would be closely involved with the welfare of such neglected and unwanted animals – but more of that anon.

▲ *The summit of Gavel Fell looking to High Stile*   ▼ *The summit of King's How looking to Skiddaw*

▲ *Blencathra from St John's in the Vale*

With the guidebooks finished and my retirement from the office imminent, I was mightily surprised to receive a letter from Harold Wilson inviting me to accept the award of MBE, without giving any reason for this honour. The Town Clerk told me in confidence that a Southport man had spent a day on the summit of Great Gable collecting signatures to a petition the object of which was to have my work on the books nationally recognised and rewarded. I thought he was pulling my leg. I received the award from the Queen: she didn't know the reason for it either. It remained a mystery for sixteen years until the Town Clerk's story was confirmed by a letter from a Southport correspondent who claimed to have known the man who stationed himself on Great Gable and was responsible for the petition. I never knew his identity.

## *Nine*

# 'RETIREMENT'

I retired from the office early in 1967, and was glad to go. I had enjoyed the work immensely but methods of accounting were changing. The days (in fact, centuries) of pen and ink accountancy in local government were numbered. Computers and calculating machines and other alleged labour-saving devices, which I could not understand, were coming in and pushing out the craftsmen. The only mechanical instrument I had in the office was a typewriter, the other work being done by hand by a staff who took pride in what they did. Pride died when the machines took over, producing unintelligible (to me) hieroglyphics that were a disgrace to the profession. Mechanics were taking the place of clerks. These were changes I could never accept. I would be useless, redundant. So I left, and although continuing to live within a mile of the office, I never went back.

◄ *Retirement*

▲ *Time to relax*

Three weeks before I left the office for good, my wife walked out of the house also for good, unable to tolerate any longer obsessions of mine that left her out in the cold, and I never saw her again. I was not greatly concerned. I had planned a very full literary programme for my years of retirement. With the series of Lakeland guidebooks finished and my duties at the office ending almost simultaneously, I could devote all my time to it, working no longer to a clock but to a calendar. I was on my own, my son being employed in Bahrain. I cut myself adrift from all my commitments and became a happy recluse in an untidy house, working nine hours a day including Sundays on books of drawings.

Concurrently I made occasional forays to the newly-opened Pennine Way, a long-distance footpath for which I had planned a guidebook; sections of it I could reach by train or bus, sometimes involving overnight stays, but the remoter parts could only conveniently be walked with the help of a car if overnight lodgings were to be avoided: I always preferred there-and-back day trips so that I could record my findings at home while they were fresh in mind. I had no car, had never had one and knew I could never hope to have the ability to drive one. Impasse!

Then a new door opened and an angel without wings appeared, offering transport; she had a car, the skill to drive it and the time to take me anywhere I wanted to go. Her name was Betty. She was small, dainty, attractive, good-looking, intelligent, well read and well informed; she was a qualified nurse and had been a teacher of speech and drama; she could pronounce long words and knew what they meant; she was fond of walking and climbing and the countryside and had a good knowledge of botany. (This compendium of attributes is my own; it has not been dictated to me.) What more could a man want? I said yes please. We went everywhere together and got on famously. Betty was manna

◀ *Working on the sketchbooks*
(© Lancashire Evening Post) ▶

from above. We were married in 1970 and, still working non-stop, I produced a stream of walkers' guidebooks to other parts of northern England and many volumes of drawings. There was something to show for every day.

When I left Blackburn in 1941 my going-away present was a small folding camera, simple to use, and I took it with me on the first tour of Scotland in 1946. I had a Freedom of Scotland railway ticket which, for £7, permitted me to travel on any of the Scottish lines for a week. I was profoundly impressed by all I saw from the carriage windows, and especially by the Highlands, which were loftier and grander than any I had seen before. They were awesome and forbidding, and wherever I went north of Glasgow they dominated every landscape, range after range coming into view and forming the far horizons, and my map told me there were many more, hundreds more, in remote areas accessible by rail or road. Gosh, I thought, what a place to explore! I knew that many men had climbed all the mountains and more aspired to do so, but for me on that first visit the prospect of setting foot on even one of them was too intimidating to contemplate: they were harsh and unfriendly, not inviting as were those at home. I was overwhelmed by the vastness of the mountain area: the Lake District, the joy of my life, was insignificant by comparison. There are four summits in Lakeland exceeding 3000 feet in height; in Scotland there are nearly three hundred.

At intermediate train halts and at the termini I could stretch my legs and they led me always towards the mountains, but I was inhibited by the railway timetables and had to be content to find good viewpoints above the valleys and take photographs of them with no thought of climbing to their tops.

I returned home to a Lakeland where the heights seemed stunted. The Highlands were infinitely grander. But I did not switch my affections. Nowhere in Scotland had I seen loveliness to compare with the Lakeland valleys nor sensed their romantic charm and the friendliness of the fells. The Highlands were grim, austere, brooding: they could not woo me away.

The following year I visited Scotland again, using the same facilities but additionally taking advantage of MacBrayne's bus services to take me into remote areas not served by the trains and into new areas of mountain grandeur. With overnight stays and ▼ *Glen Torridon*

▲ *Suilven*

miles and miles of rough walking, I could bring many of the heights within reach of my camera, but I was still too daunted by their appearance and did not venture upon them; they repelled and yet fascinated me.

These early visits set a pattern I was to follow down to the present day. For more than twenty years I returned to the Highlands regularly, and in the course of time became more adventurous, preferring fixed bases from which I could penetrate into the mountain fastnesses, climbing a few mountains on each visit and adding to my collection of photographs. But there remained areas that were quite out of bounds without personal transport.

This deficiency was remedied dramatically when Betty joined me in holy wedlock, bringing a motor car as her dowry. I introduced her to Scotland and she immediately succumbed to its appeal as I had done. Horizons widened, and landscapes hitherto hidden were revealed. We went to all parts of the country in the years that followed, not only to the remoter corners of the Highlands but across the sea to Skye and the Hebrides. I abandoned British Rail and MacBrayne's bus services, which had served me well. With a car, and not enslaved by timetables and the clock, we could reach the wild places and explore them on foot.

The Scottish mountains exceeding 3000 feet in height are called Munros after the man who first listed them, and the ascent of every one is an objective to which all red-blooded climbers aspire. I was now an old age pensioner with not more than a dozen Munros to my credit, and any slight ambition I might have had of getting to the top of all of them had faded: they were too much for me. Then I hit on the idea of at least visiting every Munro to complete my photographic collection of them and produce a comprehensive set of ink drawings of every one. Even with the help of a parked car many mountains remained hidden behind

◀ *Am Basteir,*
*Skye*

others, and it was only after long study of maps and contours and much rough walking that I brought them all within range of the camera, a mission that took me eight years of happy adventuring to complete.

I had now amassed a thousand black and white photographs of Scottish scenes, mainly of the Highlands and western seaboard. The films were processed at local chemists and, as usual, the prints were very disappointing, little care having been taken to ensure good results, much of the detail being lost. But the negatives held promise, and these I entrusted to a friend who was a professional photographer and from the consignments I passed on to him he produced most excellent enlargements which, although I say it myself, did my camera proud.

I always found that the camera gave better results in Scotland. Too often, especially in summer, the Lakeland fells are shrouded in a thin haze on successive days, but in Scotland the fine days invariably had visibility of amazing clarity. Many times from elevated viewpoints I have seen fifty-mile panoramas so clearly etched that the camera has recorded the scene faithfully.

*Ben Loyal at the head of the Kyle of Tongue*

*Meall Mheadhonach, the middle peak of Suilven*

*Stac Polly, known as 'the steep rock of the bog'*

*Cùl Mòr and Cùl Beag, mountains of Inverpolly Forest*

*Coire na Feòla, Beinn Bhàn*

*Bruach na Frithe, Skye*

*Sgùrr nan Gillean: the Pinnacle Ridge on Skye*

*Blaven and Clach Glas across Loch Slapin, Skye*

*The Black Cuillin across Loch Scavaig from Elgol, Skye*

*The island of Rhum seen to the south of Skye*

*Loch Mullardoch with the Càrn Eige range beyond*

*Loch Duich at the top of Glen Shiel*

*The Saddle seen from the Bridge of Shiel in Glen Shiel*

*The head of Loch Cluanie*

▲ *The fish sheds at Mallaig*    ▼ *Feeding time at Cluanie*

*The summit of Ben Nevis*

▲ *The Commando Memorial near Spean Bridge looking to the Ben Nevis range*     ▼ *Strath Fillan*

*The pinnacled crest of Aonach Eagach, Glen Coe*

*Ben Arthur, popularly known as The Cobbler*

▲ *Liathach across Loch Clair* ▼ *Coire Toll an Lochain, An Teallach*

▲ *Maol Chean-Dearg in Torridon* ▼ *Sgorr Ruadh in the hanging valley of Coire Lair*

The Lake District, northern England, and the Highlands and islands of Scotland have always formed my little world. I have never been abroad, never been on a ship or in an aeroplane. Why suffer passport and travel difficulties, currency problems, strange food, unintelligible language, crowded beaches, when Buttermere and Lochaber are so close at hand and so very relaxing and beautiful? The Costa del Sol is not for me.

The Lake District remains supreme in my affections. In terms of natural scenery it has not the grandeur of the Highlands, nor the underground challenge of the limestone country, nor the sweeping landscapes of the Pennines, yet surpasses all in innate loveliness, valley, lake and fell blending so sweetly in perfect harmony. There is romance in the air, magic around every corner, every vista is pleasing; all is peaceful and relaxing, the complete antidote to urban depression. But in extent, this hallowed ground is small, a paradise in miniature, and because it is small it is precious indeed, like a rare jewel it should be treasured and guarded. We should all be vigilantes.

Yet since I first saw the Lake District, discordant notes have crept into the symphony. The coming of the motor car heralded a slow decline. The authorities, to their credit, have retained the narrow valley and country roads, resisting the straightening and widening that has spoilt many a rural scene elsewhere, but have had to capitulate to car parks and caravan sites on the roadsides and the fringes of the lakes, every one not merely detracting from the scene but destroying it. New types of visitors have come. When travelling was difficult, you could be sure that the few people you met were all ardent admirers of the Lakeland scenery and there was a kinship between them. Not now. Cars and coaches throng the approach roads and unload crowds at the public toilets, gift shops and cafés. They go no further. Many are noisy, ill-mannered. Transistor radios blare out tuneless music and screaming voices. At many beauty spots pandemonium has replaced peace. Fortunately these unwelcome types have no inclination to wander out of sight of their transport; they are transient and gone by nightfall, leaving litter for others to remove. These people are completely out of tune with the surroundings and incapable of appreciating beauty.

The popular valleys of Great Langdale and Borrowdale suffer most from this modern tourist invasion: they are crowded with traffic where once there was peace. Happily there are lesser

*Fleetwith Pike from High Stile*

▲ *Town End, Troutbeck*   ▼ *Dove Cottage, Grasmere*

▲ *Bowness Bay, Windermere*

known valleys still immune from disturbance. Some of the villages too have succumbed to commercialism. Bowness was sacrificed to the day trippers long ago; Ambleside and Grasmere and Keswick are no longer places for leisurely exploration and quiet shopping. To my mind, this is very sad: the Lake District is a delicate living museum of natural beauty, unique, and should be rigorously conserved; it is not a playground nor a shopping centre.

Discerning walkers, however, still form the majority of visitors and can quickly escape to the fells and find there, on the ridges and summits, the exhilaration and freedom they seek. But even on the heights there have been minor changes. There are man-made paths where there were rough mountain tracks, and even man-made steps to ease ascents. Erosion of footpaths is a problem. Fellwalking has become a very popular pastime since the war and the number of people visiting the high places has increased a hundredfold. But erosion is not caused by too many walkers as is often assumed, but by clumsy walkers. Mountain paths were fashioned for walkers in single file, and no damage is caused by those who tread circumspectly, keeping to the original trod;

▲ *The North-Western Fells from Keswick*

indeed they help to firm the ground. Damage is caused by parties of three or four trying to walk abreast and maintain conversation: they kick the verges away and loosen stones and make an untidy widening of the path. The worst offenders are parties of school-children, often too many in number to keep under control, who treat the paths as playgrounds, kicking and throwing stones, romping over the verges and generally having fun. The grown-ups in charge should be more responsible. Solitary walkers are excused from blame: they keep strictly to the trodden ways, travel in silence as everybody should on the fells, appreciating all they see without the distractions of conversation. They are the true disciples of the pioneers. And there are evidences of vandalism. A few summit cairns, memorials to their builders, have been wantonly scattered.

These annoyances, however, are no more than pin pricks and probably noticeable only to those who knew the fells fifty or sixty years ago and treated them with reverence. In general the high places have remained inviolate and still offer, as always, the pleasure and the excitement of joyful days of exercise and adventure, and the satisfaction of reaching a difficult summit as a

*▲ The old parish church of Bassenthwaite*

reward for arduous effort. Such days for me and many others were the best days of our lives. They were the best remedies for a bad week in the office or the factory. Carefree days of complete bliss far above the world and its worries and, of course, the fells look down on a Lakeland as beautiful and charming as ever it was, with valleys and lakes in glorious array. Up here, Lakeland has not changed: the superlative views and panoramas are exactly the same. The wild fellsides will never be tamed. The discordant elements of the valleys are out of sight and sound. All around is an exquisite fairyland that brings tears of happiness.

An old lady of eighty-four, after her first tour of the district, bettered Wordsworth by saying simply, 'God must spend his holidays here.'

In latter years, I suffered from much unsought publicity. It all started after the BBC announced their intention to make a TV programme about me. I declined to appear but the programme went ahead, the producer interviewing a few people who knew me, all of them speaking in the past tense as though contributing to an obituary, and finally I had to show myself briefly to correct

*Grasmoor seen across Crummock Water from Mellbreak*

*The top of the Napes, Great Gable*

*Great Gable and Pillar from Glaramara*

*▲ AW at Kapellan, the animal refuge near Kendal*

this impression. The programme sparked off a national interest that amazed me, bringing a spate of correspondence, many requests for press interviews and a generous offer from a leading London publisher.

It then occurred to me that, as a result of this interest, new and lucrative sources of income could be earned for a local animal welfare charity of which I was Chairman. For ten years a hard-working and dedicated committee had been saving funds with the object of establishing a shelter where homeless and straying cats and dogs could be cared for until new owners could be found for them: an ambition that seemed to be unattainable and was described by critics as 'pie in the sky'. A bonanza followed. The first windfall was provided by the Westmorland Gazette, publishers of all my books thus far, who bought the copyrights for a sum so substantial that the Charity was able to purchase a very attractive country property near Kendal and establish a refuge for distressed animals. Additionally, large donations from the publishers, Michael Joseph, in lieu of royalties, and some bequests and legacies, were sufficient to create a six-figure endowment fund and make the financial future of the Charity secure. I have sacrificed my image as a very private person, but the end has justified the means.

I wouldn't mind living the last eighty years again, every day having held interest for me. But I am glad I shall not be here to live through the next eighty. I feel sorry for posterity. The world is sick, and getting worse. Moral standards and strict disciplines have gone to seed. Few seem to care two hoots about the old virtues of pride and dependability and respect for others. Violence and terrorism and vandalism are rampant. Clever men are engaged in devising instruments of mass destruction. The world is not only sick, but mad.

We have gone soft. Forgiveness for irresponsible actions, appeals for better conduct, wagging fingers of admonition, trifling fines and suspended prison sentences are ineffective against the rising surge of crime. The police, the friends of society, have their hands tied by timid legislation, and are reviled and abused. The only deterrent for violence is physical pain. The culprits should be birched until they squeal for the mercy they denied their victims. Football hooliganism would be cured overnight if the penalty was castration. National Service should be brought back for the layabouts who cause trouble and have never been subject to iron discipline. We let vicious criminals live in furnished cells and be waited on by public servants, the cost being paid by the society they have wilfully injured. Off with their heads! Religion proclaims a cure for all the ills of mankind but has turned sour; stupid peoples of different faiths and dogmas are slaughtering each other all over the world. The church advocates tolerance but takes sides and cannot stop the carnage. Refugee camps proliferate. The Sermon on the Mount is a dead duck.

The be-and and end-all of life for so many people is the making of money, a pursuit commendable insofar as it leads to a comfortable independence, but so often it goes far beyond and becomes an exercise in amassing wealth. Money may not be the root of all evil but it accounts for a lot of it. I have never agreed with parents who build up a fortune for their children to inherit, having seen too many young people of promise become lazy and indolent by sudden wealth. Children should make their own way in the world, build character and succeed on their merits. The present generation is not helped by offers of loans for trivial purposes and inducements to enter into commitments they cannot

*Green Crag and Haystacks, with Pillar behind*

*Haystacks and the High Stile range from Grey Knotts*

afford. I consider the banks in particular to be highly immoral in their efforts, widely advertised, to persuade their customers to accept loans to cover sundry expenses, even holidays, when their advice should be to urge them to save money until they have sufficient for the proposed outlay, as always used to be the case. The banks should stop saying yes. Personal possessions should be one's own and paid for. There is satisfaction in saying 'This is my own, earned by my own efforts.' There is none in admitting debts.

But enough of griping and grousing; I did not intend the book to end on a catalogue of criticisms and grumbles. I have been described recently as being crusty and intolerant in my old age. I am not, really, but I did want to get a few niggles off my chest before signing off. In fact, I have very little personal interest in what is going on in the world; I am a detached observer, not involved, keeping everybody and everything at arm's length. I am unperturbed by wars and have no time at all for party politics. My hackles rise only when I hear of cruelty to animals. Man's cruelty to man it not my concern. I live in a shell of my own making. Betty is my defence against intruders, and now my eyes.

# Ten

# WHEN THE MIND'S EYE
# TAKES OVER

If I spent the rest of my life telling of my memories of the fells, time would defeat me. There are so many. Some are still vivid in the mind, some have become dreamy with the passing years. But all are pleasant, and many beautiful. There were days of drenching rain, but I was always content to spend time in the lee of boulder or crags, watching the rise and fall of the mists. The first drop of cold water that gets through your defences and runs an erratic course down your ribs is always the worst: those that follow matter less. You can get wet through to the skin, and yet glow with health. There were days of perishing cold, when I huddled by summit cairns and made notes with hands turned blue and stiff, but five minutes' walking brought back a tingling warmth. There were days of fierce wind, a worse enemy than rain or cold; then climbing a mountain meant fighting a battle, too: a battle that left me not weak but strong, for these tussles with the elements do a power of good, freeing the mind from worldly worries and strengthening the body. I caught many a bad cold at the office, never a one on the hills. Snow was a more subtle adversary. It transforms the fells into fields of dazzling whiteness and the distant scene into a fairy wonderland. It is beautiful; beautiful, but treacherous. Snow is feminine, a temptress: when you meet her, watch your step. When her seduction hardens into ice, avoid her. The fells are best left alone after frost. And in thunderstorms.

But it is the warm sunny days that remain most clearly etched in the memory: the beautiful days of blue skies and dappled clouds; the quiet days when rain and wind slunk away, seemingly for ever; the lazy days when life held no greater joy than to lie on the ground and idly listen to the music of a tumbling stream, soft

*Unnamed tarn on Haystacks, with High Crag behind*

*Crummock Water from High Stile*

*▶ Ashness Bridge looking across to Derwentwater*

music with never a discord, and watch the dramas being played by moving pinheads in the grass. There was another world of activity here and life was exciting: there were bullies and cowards and heroes, and eager lovers and swooning females.

But most of all, it is the bewitching beauty of Lakeland that haunts the mind, as the daffodils of Ullswater haunted Wordsworth: scenes that pass across the inward eye as a pageant of loveliness. Not so much the scenes preferred by the tourists – Ashness Bridge, Friar's Crag, Orrest Head – charming though they are, but the unexpected scenes, those revealed by a movement of mist, those that dramatically come into view on the last few steps to a summit cairn, those that stop a walker in his tracks as he rounds a corner and glimpses a picture beautiful beyond belief, those that occur in early morning when the sun breaks through the mist over the valley, or in the evening when one is loth to leave the peace of the tops and enjoys the reward of perfect sunsets. Or the memories in miniature, the more intimate charm of sparkling waterfalls in ferny dells, of winter birches touched by sunlight against a dark sky, of squirrels running along a wall, of trees laden with new snow, of translucent waters in rocky pools,

*▲ The Fairfield Horseshoe from Wansfell Pike*

of lonely rowans splashing grey rocks with vivid colour, of hovering buzzards motionless in the sky and ravens in tumbling flight, of wood-smoke rising lazily from farm chimneys in the quiet of evening, of sheepdogs watching intently every movement of their masters and refusing to be distracted, of newborn lambs and their proud mothers. Oh, a pen cannot tell of these joys. A walk in Lakeland is a walk in heaven.

Mountain climbing satisfies an instinct all men should feel: the urge to get to the top. It is natural for a man to look up, to strive to attain something higher and out of his immediate reach, to overcome the difficulties and disappointments of his upward progress, to exult at his ultimate success. Mountain climbing is an epitome of life, and good practice for it. You start at the bottom, the weaklings and the irresolute drop out on the way up, the determined reach the top. Life is like that.

Days on the fells have always been for me the best days of all. They still are, but now I must be content to relive them in memories; my sight is failing but I can visualise past adventures so clearly in the eye of the mind. I can sit in an armchair and go up Great Gable again, or cross Mickledore to Scafell, and the pictures

*The Buttermere Fells from the summit of Mellbreak*

*The Scafell range from the summit of Pillar*

*Pillar and Scoat Fell across Ennerdale Water*

◀ *Napes Needle,*
*Great Gable*

I see with closed eyes are as vivid as they ever were. What a blessing is memory when a happy life is coming to a close; what pleasure there is in recalling days of enjoyment and exhilaration! The good times live on to the end.

Don't get me wrong. I have no complaints, none at all. I have had a long and wonderful innings and enjoyed a remarkable immunity from unpleasant and unwelcome incidents. Events have always moved to my advantage. So much could have gone wrong but hasn't. I never had to go to be a soldier, which I would have hated. I never had to wear a uniform, which I would also have loathed. I was never called upon to make speeches in public nor forced into the limelight; my role was that of a backroom boy, which suited me fine. I never went bald, which would have driven me into hiding: I see so many men who have lost their hair and seem not to care a damn, but to me it would have been a major tragedy. Most of all, I have enjoyed perfect health, despite smoking like a chimney since the age of sixteen. I have never had a serious illness, never had an accident, never had an operation. For forty-seven years I worked in local government without losing a day or even an hour through sickness. I enjoyed my work so much that the thought of feigning a reason for absence never once occurred to me. As I have said earlier, of things mechanical I am innocent, having no knowledge at all; ignoramus would be a better word. I simply do not understand how gadgets and contraptions work. I have always been excused household duties because of incompetence; the only tool I can use with success is a pen. Mechanics are an unsolved mystery. Continuous frustration has made me a firm advocate of Murphy's Law (if a thing can go wrong, it will). But here too when grappling with a dilemma there has always been someone around who says, 'Get out of the way. Let me show you how to do it.' I watch but nothing

▶ *Watendlath*

▲ *Mirklin Cove, Scoat Fell*  ▼ *Scafell Crag*

▶ *Pike o'Blisco*

registers. So, all told, I have enjoyed a charmed life. I have been well favoured. The gods have smiled on me since the cradle. I have had more blessings than I could ever count.

Louis Armstrong used to tell us that this is a wonderful world. He was right. It is. We should all feel privileged to live amid such bounty. We should all be joyously happy. All around us, or within each reach, are Nature's exquisite pageants in a country-side richly endowed with delights: gardens of flowers, fragrant meadows, lovely trees where birds sing, chuckling streams winding the tapestries of enchanting valleys below the colourful backcloth of hills. There is beauty everywhere: in the humble daisy, in the dappling of sunlight in woodland glades, in the clouds, everywhere. There are the miracles of renewal, sunset marking the end of a day and dawn heralding the start of another. And the marvels of the changing seasons: springtime bursting into new life after the long sleep of winter, high summer followed by the slow death of autumn. We live in a magical fairyland of subtle charm and it is given to us to enjoy as an absolute gift. You do not need money in your pocket to walk through a field of wild flowers or on a heather moor. It is a gift we do little to deserve. I

*▲ Haystacks   ▼ Great Gable from Kirk Fell*

simply cannot understand people who complain of depression when there is so much beauty and pleasure available to them in our parks and gardens. I think they should be given a rose to study, or better still, instead of taking their daily dosage of pills, ordered to climb Helvellyn by way of Striding Edge: I am sure they would come down mentally refreshed and possibly cured.

Louis was absolutely right. It is a wonderful world. We have more blessings than we could ever count.

My space is nearly finished. I could have used it better, but the words that would more adequately tell the glory of the fells are not known to me. Like a lover who can only keep repeating the same three words because there are no others that say more, I have found the pen, in my hands, no instrument for describing the captivating charm of Lakeland. Lakeland is an emotion, and emotions are felt, not expressed.

I will end by wishing you many many happy days on the fells. You will be following in my footsteps, wherever you go, and I hope you find the enjoyment I found: I am sure you will. Please be helpful to the people you meet, and please be kind to the birds and animals. Forgive my saying it just one more time: don't forget to watch where you are putting your feet, and you'll be all right.

I can't expect to last much longer. My sisters and my brother have passed on, dying in the order in which they were born, all in their eighties. My turn next. I shall be sorry to go and leave behind a world I have enjoyed living in, a world of wonders, despoiled in parts by man but still a realm of infinite delight, free to all mankind equally.

This book is not a personal lament for the end of fellwalking and the end of active life, but a thanksgiving for the countless blessings that have been mine in the last eighty years. All I ask for, at the end, is a last long resting place by the side of Innominate Tarn, on Haystacks, where the water gently laps the gravelly shore and the heather blooms and Pillar and Gable keep unfailing watch. A quiet place, a lonely place. I shall go to it, for the last time, and be carried: someone who knew me in life will take me and empty me out of a little box and leave me there alone.

And if you, dear reader, should get a bit of grit in your boot as you are crossing Haystacks in the years to come, please treat it with respect. It might be me.

*Innominate Tarn, Haystacks*

# BIBLIOGRAPHY OF
# A. WAINWRIGHT'S WORKS

A Pictorial Guide to the Lakeland Fells

1. *Book One*: The Eastern Fells   1955
2. *Book Two*: The Far Eastern Fells   1957
3. *Book Three*: The Central Fells   1958
4. *Book Four*: The Southern Fells   1960
5. *Book Five*: The Northern Fells   1962
6. *Book Six*: The North Western Fells   1964
7. *Book Seven*: The Western Fells   1966

8. Fellwanderer: *The Story behind the Guidebooks*   1966
9. Pennine Way Companion   1968
10. A Lakeland Sketchbook   1969
11. Walks in Limestone Country   1970
12. A Second Lakeland Sketchbook   1970
13. A Third Lakeland Sketchbook   1971
14. Walks on the Howgill Fells   1972
15. A Fourth Lakeland Sketchbook   1972
16. A Coast to Coast Walk: *St Bees Head to Robin Hood's Bay*   1973
17. A Fifth Lakeland Sketchbook   1973
18. The Outlying Fells of Lakeland   1974

Scottish Mountain Drawings

19. *Volume One*: The Northern Highlands   1974
20. *Volume Two*: The North-Western Highlands   1976
21. *Volume Three*: The Western Highlands   1976
22. *Volume Four*: The Central Highlands   1977
23. *Volume Five*: The Eastern Highlands   1978
24. *Volume Six*: The Islands   1979

25. Westmorland Heritage   1974
26. A Dales Sketchbook   1976
27. Kendal in the Nineteenth Century   1977

28. A Second Dales Sketchbook   1978
29. A Furness Sketchbook   1978
30. Walks from Ratty   1978
31. A Second Furness Sketchbook   1979
32. Three Westmorland Rivers   1979
33. A Lune Sketchbook   1980
34. A Ribble Sketchbook   1980
35. An Eden Sketchbook   1980

Lakeland Mountain Drawings
36. *Volume One*      1980
37. *Volume Two*      1981
38. *Volume Three*    1982
39. *Volume Four*     1983
40. *Volume Five*     1984

41. Welsh Mountain Drawings   1981
42. A Bowland Sketchbook   1981
43. A North Wales Sketchbook   1982
44. A Wyre Sketchbook   1982
45. A South Wales Sketchbook   1983
46. A Peak District Sketchbook   1984
47. Wainwright in Lakeland   1985
48. Old Roads of Eastern Lakeland   1985
49. Ex-Fellwanderer   1987
50. Fellwalking with a Camera   1988

51. Fellwalking with Wainwright   1984
    *with photographs by Derry Brabbs*
52. Wainwright on the Pennine Way   1985
    *with photographs by Derry Brabbs*
53. A Pennine Journey   1986
54. Wainwright's Coast to Coast Walk   1987
    *with photographs by Derry Brabbs*
55. Wainwright in Scotland   1988
    *with photographs by Derry Brabbs*
56. Wainwright on the Lakeland Mountain Passes   1989
    *with photographs by Derry Brabbs*
57. Wainwright in the Limestone Dales   1991
    *with photographs by Ed Geldard*
58. Wainwright's Favourite Lakeland Mountains   1991
    *with photographs by Derry Brabbs*
59. Wainwright in the Valleys of Lakeland   1992
    *with photographs by Derry Brabbs*

# Index

Italic numbers refer to illustrations